How to cope after relationship abuse for women

Janet Haines
Mandy Matthewson

Acknowledgements:
Steven Haines
Robyn Cartledge
Coverart designed by Freepik
(www.freepik.com)

This workbook offers suggestions on how to cope in the aftermath of an abusive relationship. We do not guarantee that these suggested strategies will resolve all psychological symptoms. You may wish to seek alternative assistance from a mental health professional.

How to cope after relationship abuse for women
Janet Haines & Mandy Matthewson
Copyright © 2025
ISBN: 978-1-923573-10-9

About the authors

Dr Janet Haines has a PhD in Clinical Psychology and has worked as an academic and researcher for 17 years, and in private practice for 30 years helping people facing life problems.

Dr Mandy Matthewson is a Clinical Psychologist, educator and researcher with more than two decades of experience supporting people through life's toughest challenges.

For A, who chose to speak up despite the risk.
Your courage made you safe.
For L, who was cautious about speaking out because of the risk.
Your prudence kept you safe.

Table of contents

- Introduction 8
- The nature of abuse and how it affects you 9
  - Physical assault 9
  - Sexual abuse 10
  - Threats and intimidation/bullying 11
  - Coercion 12
  - Verbal abuse 13
  - Humiliation 14
  - Social isolation 15
  - Abduction/deprivation of liberty 16
  - Stalking 17
  - Economic/financial abuse 18
- The cycle of abuse 21
  - The four stages of the abuse cycle 21
  - What is the impact of this cycle of abuse? 22
- Why did I stay? 23
  - A complicated issue 23
  - I was too scared to leave 23
  - He said he would kill himself if I left 24
  - But I loved him… 25
  - The abuser's expressions of regret and promises of change 26
  - There were children involved 27
  - Loss of sense of self-efficacy and self-confidence 28
  - Low sense of self-worth 28
  - Lack of social support 29
- The issue of gaslighting 31
  - Types of gaslighting 31
  - What should I be looking for? 34
  - Indicators of gaslighting and the effects on you 40
- My reaction to the end of the relationship 42
  - The abuser ended the relationship 42
  - You ended the relationship 42
  - Grief and disenfranchised grief 42
- What do I need to do now? 46
- Keep yourself safe 48

- Manage your anxiety/trauma 50
  - What is your nervous system doing? 50
  - Range of arousal 52
  - Anxiety management strategies 54
  - Quietening your mind 61
- Dealing with sleep disturbance 67
  - What can I do about my sleep problems? 69
- Regulating your emotions 71
  - Recognising and dealing with your emotions 72
  - The link between your emotions and your behaviour 75
- Learn to cope 78
  - Problem-focused coping vs. emotion-focused coping 78
  - Identifying your preferred coping style 81
  - Building your coping repertoire 85
- Fix your thinking 95
  - How are our thoughts affected? 95
  - Core beliefs 96
  - Cognitive errors 96
  - Why do we think in unhelpful ways? 107
  - Underlying assumptions of logical errors 109
  - Understanding automatic thoughts 112
  - Catching automatic thoughts 112
  - Understanding and noticing logical errors 114
  - Reframing your thoughts (cognitive restructuring) 117
  - Making the restructured thinking habitual 121
  - Targeting the assumptions 121
- Re-establish a sense of self and self-worth 126
  - Factors that enhance a sense of self and self-worth 126
  - How to build self-worth 127
  - Thoughts and beliefs to promote high self-worth 129
- Re-build your self-efficacy 130
  - The concept of self-efficacy 130
  - The link between self-efficacy and relationship abuse 130
  - Why is self-efficacy important? 130
  - Ways to improve self-efficacy 131
- Understand your rights 137
- Learn to be assertive 141

    Asking for change 141
    Negotiating for what you want 144
Improving the quality of your life 146
    Values clarification exercise for choosing preferred activities 146
Some final points 149
Additional readings 151

Introduction

This workbook has been written to help you cope with the recovery period after the end of an abusive relationship where you have been the target of your partner's abuse. We have focused on that time after the end of the relationship and not during the relationship for a couple of reasons.

Firstly, it is often the case that during an abusive relationship, you are in what we would label survival mode. You put one foot in front of the other to get through the day and have little time or headspace to consider your situation, how you feel, and what to do. It is like being in an almost permanent crisis state. When you are focusing on handling a crisis, you do not have the capacity to care about your longer-term needs, including your mental health needs. You just try to hold things together because you have no choice but to do so.

Secondly, it is damaging to you to be in an abusive relationship. This is true from both a physical and psychological point of view. It is not easy to deal with that damage while the harm is still occurring. After the end of the relationship, your recovery needs that will promote your well-being can receive some attention without the interference of ongoing abuse.

In this book, the focus is on the recovery from the abuse and the damage it has caused you. However, it may be helpful to consider the self-help options available to you at a time when you are considering leaving.

In this workbook, we are going to go over some aspects of abuse in a relationship because it is important for you to understand the nature of the influences on you and the ways you have been affected. Then, we will focus on the things you can do to help yourself in your recovery from the abusive relationship.

This workbook does not replace the need for a therapeutic relationship with a psychologist or counsellor who can help you through this recovery process. It is designed to offer ways to help yourself and encourage you to see that recovery is possible.

The nature of abuse and how it affects you

Here, we are going to consider different ways in which abuse manifests in a relationship and how each type of abuse can affect you. It is worth pointing out that there are other ways abuse in a relationship can present itself, and you can probably identify some of those other forms of abuse from your own experiences. An important point is that each new type of abuse does not necessarily have a different effect on you. There are some commonalities in the challenges that the various forms of abuse can cause.

Physical assault

What is it?

Using the term assault, we refer to any form of physical attack, whether or not it causes physical injury. In this way, assault ranges from behaviours such as pushing and shoving up to physical assault that causes grievous bodily harm that can result in life-changing and life-threatening injuries.

Whether or not medical assistance is sought in the aftermath of a physical assault cannot be used as a reliable indicator of the seriousness of the assault. Some people do not seek medical help for the injuries they sustain. This may be due to not wishing to be questioned about how the injuries occurred or the perpetrator of the abuse preventing the injured person from seeking medical attention. We have met people who have had bones broken as a result of relationship abuse but have not sought medical help or have been prevented from having their broken bones set.

> *Sarah arrived for her first therapy session. She was well dressed and quietly spoken. It was clear that her left wrist was severely deformed. In the course of giving an account of her relationship experiences, Sarah said her abusive boyfriend had broken her wrist. She said he had forcibly and deliberately broken her arm and then refused to allow her to seek medical assistance. Sarah said she was too scared to go behind his back and seek medical care. She feared that if he learned that she had sought help, he would harm her more severely. Sarah recounted that in subsequent physical attacks, her boyfriend would deliberately target her left wrist, knowing that it would cause her pain. When recounting these events, her demeanour did not change. She spoke quietly, politely and matter-of-factly.*

It is not unusual for people who do seek medical attention for injuries caused by physical assault in a relationship to give an incorrect account of the cause of the injury to medical personnel. This is not about, or not only about, protecting the perpetrator of the abuse. It is more likely about protecting themselves from the reaction of the abuser to their disclosure to medical personnel about the true nature of the abuse.

How does it affect you?

By living in an environment where you can be physically attacked and harmed at any time, that environment becomes unsafe and unpredictable. This causes you to be in a permanent state of hypervigilance where you are on the lookout for signs that physical harm is imminent. So, you come to be in a permanent state of nervous system arousal. You become very sensitive to any signs of threat and experience a constant state of anxiety.

You also end up existing in a constant state of conflict between protecting the abuser and your relationship and protecting yourself. If you choose to defend yourself, you end up causing problems for the perpetrator and, potentially, damaging the relationship on which you have become dependent. The perpetrator and the unhealthy relationship often come out on top in this conflict. With your needs always being given the least consideration, you can come to value yourself as less important than the abuser or the maintenance of the relationship.

Sexual abuse

What is it?

Part of the experience of sexual abuse is sexual attack, that is, forced sexual intercourse that in this, as in other contexts, is considered to be rape. The fact that it takes place within an existing relationship does not change the nature of this type of attack. Without consent, sexual intercourse is still forced and unwanted.

As well as this type of assault, sexual abuse can be experienced in other forms that are still abusive. For example, sexual abuse can involve you being coerced into engaging in sexual behaviour that is unwanted by you or that is degrading to you. You might agree to engage in the behaviour to please your partner or because you have been encouraged by the abuser to believe you have an obligation to do this, but if you were given a genuine choice, it is not what you would have chosen to do.

Another problem that can arise is how an abusive partner can use sexual activity. For example, sexual behaviour can be used as a form of punishment by the abuser, either by withholding sexual intimacy or forcing unwanted sexual activity in response to a perceived wrongdoing on your part. The use of sexual activity in this way by the abuser does not rely on you having done anything wrong, only that the abuser believes you deserve punishment.

Another way in which the abuser can use sexual interactions with the abuser is through linking it with other negative interactions, such as a physical attack. For example, a severe episode of physical abuse can be followed by an aggressive sexual interaction, even in cases where you were physically injured and in pain.

> *When describing what she had experienced, Alicia said her partner would physically assault her and then would want to engage in sexual intercourse. She said he would become enraged and hurt her badly. She said she would be bleeding, swollen, in pain and crying, and her partner would then demand sexual intercourse. She described how her partner seemed to become sexually aroused by his attack on her and her pain and suffering. She said these episodes were the lowest points in her relationship with this person.*

How does this affect you?

Having your physical and psychological integrity threatened sexually is a personal violation that can be intolerable for most people and can be traumatic in nature. It denies you the ability to control what is happening to you. In general, having little control in your life is anxiety-provoking and damages your sense of self and who you are.

Such treatment can cause you to become confused about the nature of relationships and distort your views about the distinction between love and abuse. Loving feelings should not be expressed in harmful ways, so it is not surprising that a deep sense of uncertainty about your worthiness as a lovable person develops.

Threats and intimidation/bullying

What is it?

Physical attacks and unwanted sexual activity are not necessary components of abuse. It is an emotionally abusive act to threaten such behaviour. This might be in the form of direct physical harm, such as a threat to break your arm or punch you in the face. However, the danger may also be indirect, with a suggestion of harm. An example would be that you will "get what is coming to you". There is no direct statement of what will happen, but you know it will be bad.

The threats may not only be directed towards you. To indirectly threaten you and force you to do what the abuser wants, the abuser may threaten others who are important to you. This may be done directly (e.g., "I will beat up your mother") or indirectly (e.g., "Your mother will have to spend the rest of her life looking over her shoulder").

> *Rachael discussed the responsibility she had felt to protect her younger sister from harm. She said she did not stand up to her abusive partner because of his constant threats that if she did not do as he wished, he would rape her sister. Rachael's sister was a teenager, and the thought of her partner hurting her was more than Rachael could tolerate. Given all the things he had done to Rachael, she did not doubt for a moment that he would follow through with his threats if he decided he would do so. Even now, after their relationship had ended, Rachael was not confident that her ex-partner would not harm her sister just because he wanted to punish Rachael. She lived in fear.*

Threats and other forms of intimidation and bullying are aimed at controlling your behaviour. They encourage you to become and remain compliant with the wishes of the abuser. The goal is to get you to do something you would otherwise not choose to do if you had not been threatened, intimidated or bullied.

How does this affect you?

In the same way that an actual physical attack can cause you to be threat-sensitive and in a constant state of fear, to some degree, so does the threat of harm. You live in a state of alertness, looking for signs that the threat of harm will change to actual harm.

Further, when the threat is directed towards others you care about, you can take on board a sense of responsibility for the wellbeing of these people that is beyond what is reasonable. Given that you have very little control over what the abuser chooses to do, you end up worrying about things that you cannot influence. You keep trying to adjust your own behaviour to protect others even though there is no real way of doing so.

Coercion

What is this?

Abusive partners will use emotional manipulation to get you to do things you would otherwise not choose to do. Coercion can also be used to get you to abandon issues you would much prefer to confront, but the abuser does not want to be raised.

Abusers tend to focus on your greatest fears and vulnerabilities when coercing you into doing what they want. They take advantage of your emotional state, which has already been affected by other abusive experiences. You will feel you have no choice but to do what they expect. It is like being put in an impossible situation you cannot win.

> *When Melissa began a relationship with her abusive partner, she had two children from a previous relationship. Her attempts at co-parenting with the children's father had been fraught with difficulties. Knowing this, Melissa's current, abusive partner threatened to tell Melissa's former partner of fabricated poor parenting behaviours by Melissa if she did not do as he demanded. The list of things he wanted was endless and Melissa could never predict what he would want next. Whatever she did was never good enough, and he would again threaten Melissa's relationship with her children, claiming that if he told the children's father what a terrible mother she was, she would lose custody of her children. Although Melissa knew that what he was claiming about her parenting was false, she feared losing her children. As a result, she felt forced to give in to his demands.*

How does this affect you?

This type of coercion and emotional manipulation is psychologically damaging. It causes you to feel intense anxiety. It can make you feel helpless (i.e., nothing you can do to change things) and hopeless about the future (i.e., nothing will ever change). Feelings of helplessness and hopelessness are linked to feelings of depressed mood.

The use of coercion and emotional manipulation can strengthen the power imbalance in the relationship that is already in favour of the abuser. This type of power imbalance results in you feeling like you have little control over what happens to you and never feeling like your concerns are listened to or your needs met. It creates feelings of worthlessness and lack of value.

Verbal abuse

What is this?

Verbal abuse refers to a stream of derogatory rants directed at you by the abusive partner. This abuse may take the form of shouting but also may be quietly spoken. Its main characteristic is its unrelenting nature. Once triggered, the verbal abuse can persist for extended periods, wearing you down until you give in or shut down.

It is important to know that this type of abuse typically is not triggered by any wrongdoing on your part or, at least, not sufficiently severe that it would warrant it. More likely, verbal abuse by the abuser is related to the abuser's personal characteristics, their behaviour or their displeasure based on their own interpretation of what is happening at that time.

> *Caitlin used to dread the tirades she had to endure from her abusive partner. Once he started, he could go on and on about how unfair it was that he had to put up with someone like her, how she was not as good as any number of other people he would mention, how she had done things wrong, and how unhappy she made him, for example. Just when she thought it was ending, he would start again, ranting and raving about her perceived shortcomings. When she felt she couldn't cope with anymore, she would realise he was only just getting started. Sometimes, she would receive a brief tongue-lashing, but other times, the verbal abuse could go on for days.*

How does this affect you?

The unrelenting nature of the verbal abuse and its negative content is damaging to you. The constant barrage of abuse can cause you to change the way you view yourself. Like other forms of abuse, it encourages feelings of low self-worth. In addition, this type of abuse can change how you view the world, how it works, and how you fit into it. The world seems to be a riskier and more threatening place than might otherwise be the case.

This type of abuse can cause you to feel sensitive to signs of threat. This is both because the abuse is targeted at you and, often, your integrity, but also because it is unpredictable regarding when it will occur. This is because it is usually unrelated to any action on your part. It can seemingly come out of the blue.

Further, one particular difficulty is knowing when it will end. There may be lulls in the tirade, followed by the abuser returning to the ranting abuse. In fact, victims of this type of abuse often have labelled it as more distressing than physical abuse. Typically, with physical abuse, there will be a point when the abuse starts and a definite point where that episode of abuse ends. That is, when it is over, you know that the physical abuse is finished for that time. In contrast, verbal abuse can drag on for hours or even days.

Humiliation

What is it?

This refers to a type of abuse, the purpose of which is to cause you to feel humiliated. This might be achieved by the abuser engaging in specific actions (e.g., demanding that you wear unflattering clothing) or by the content of what is said to you (e.g., calling you demeaning names). The humiliation may be caused by experiences that take place in private, or it may be carried out by the abusive partner in public settings, causing you to feel humiliated in front of others.

> *Helena's abusive partner had a habit of making comments to his friends about the most intimate aspects of their relationship. He would describe features of her body in a degrading way. He would make unflattering comparisons with other women he would identify as being more attractive than Helena. He thought his comments were hilarious, and he would laugh about her, and his friends would join in, seemingly appreciating his 'humour'. All of this would take place in Helena's presence. She always felt humiliated. Showing any sign she was upset by his behaviour would cause him to escalate his attempts to humiliate her with a cruelty that was damaging to her.*

How does this affect you?

Being constantly humiliated can change the way you view yourself. You may come to see yourself as less worthwhile, which influences the decisions you make that affect you. These changes can affect your self-confidence and self-efficacy.

Further, constant humiliation that affects the way you view yourself also leaves you vulnerable to these experiences altering how you feel. Mood changes are a common consequence of viewing yourself in a poor light.

Social isolation

What is it?

Social isolation as a form of abuse involves your abusive partner preventing you from speaking to or spending time with family and friends. This may occur directly, where you are forbidden from contacting your loved ones, or indirectly through discouraging you from having this contact or punishing you for even raising the possibility of spending time with your family or friends.

> *Lisa's abusive partner never came out and directly told her not to see her family, but she got the message anyway. Although he didn't really know her family members, he was always critical of them when talking to Lisa. When she told him what they had said about ordinary matters, he would dispute the veracity of their comments, claiming they didn't know what they were talking about... on any topic. Early on in the relationship, whenever she mentioned she would see her family members, her partner's disapproval was written all over his face. Then, as time went on, it became apparent to Lisa that if she saw her family, she would be punished by her partner. Sometimes, he wouldn't speak to her for days. Other times, he would physically assault her if his mood was bad enough. Lisa quickly learned to distance herself from her family.*

In addition, the abusive partner might try to diminish your loved ones in your eyes. This might be achieved by telling you that your family and friends think poorly of you or that they have said negative things about your partner, causing you to support your partner over the other significant people in your life.

Alternatively, your abusive partner may have told your family and friends negative things about you to cause them to withdraw their support from you. It does not matter if what they are told is not valid, their withdrawal of support causes you to be more socially isolated.

How does this affect you?

The purpose of this form of abuse is to isolate you from those who could help you or those who would offer you a frame of reference that is different from the one the abuser is presenting to you. For example, if the abuser wants you to believe they are in control and you are wrong in the way you are looking at their behaviour, they do not want others to offer you a different story than the one they are presenting.

As the abuser limits your view, you develop a smaller and more limited version of how the world works. It then becomes harder and harder to challenge this version. You then adopt your abusive partner's version of reality as your own. In your abusive partner's version, you are lacking in all ways, so you come to see yourself as lacking.

Abduction/deprivation of liberty

What is this?

In a move to deprive you of any power in the relationship and make sure the abuser is in control, you may have your ability to move freely taken away from you. This may be in the form of removing you to a different location where you know no one and from which you do not have the means to return.

You may be locked up in a room within the house or an outbuilding on your home property. Your release from these locked locations is in the control of the abuser and not up to you.

> *Before escaping the relationship, Georgia spent long periods locked in a shed on the property where she lived with her partner. She spent most of her time in this small space for the last few months of the relationship. She was allowed out to use the bathroom only when her partner allowed it. He told her she had not earned the right to walk around free because of her poor behaviour, although Georgia had never learned what she had done wrong. When she was let out of the shed, she was so grateful that she found herself thanking her partner for his kindness. At times, she knew what was happening was terrible. However, she stopped listening to that internal voice for the rest of the time.*

However, the deprivation of your liberty may not require that you be locked up or removed to an isolated location. The abusive partner may instil in you an understanding that you must not and cannot move beyond the limits set by the abuser without their permission. An example is the young woman who, at the direction of her then-partner, would sit at the end of the bed with her chin on her chest, sometimes for hours. She would stay there until she was given permission to move. She would not move even if her abusive partner was not present in the home because she knew the consequences if she was found to have moved without his permission.

How does this affect you?

This type of abuse reflects a severe power imbalance in the relationship. Depriving you of your liberty makes you feel powerless and lacking in control over your own life. It gives the abuser too much power that is wielded with disregard for your well-being.

Depriving you of the freedom to come and go as you please reduces your chances of obtaining help or exposing you to different frames of reference about how other, non-abusive relationships work.

Also, depriving you of the freedom to make choices for yourself limits your life and makes it small. You live the life your abusive partner allows you but not the one you might want if circumstances were different. It is easy to accept that you do not deserve the sort of life other people take for granted.

Stalking

What is it?

Here, we are referring to abusive behaviour where your partner keeps track of your every move, where you are and who you are with. This can take a number of forms, but all involve checking up on you and knowing what you are doing.

This type of abuse may take the form of your abusive partner checking your phone to see who you have contacted or who has contacted you. Any evidence that you have done something that displeases your partner is used as evidence of your wrongdoing, even if the other person is the one who contacted you or nothing untoward was discussed. In the same way, your Internet and social media use can be monitored.

Your location can be monitored in person or with a GPS locator placed on your car or a GPS app used on your phone. In this way, wherever you are located can be identified at any point in time by your abusive partner.

It may also be the case that you can be physically followed. This can be done by your abusive partner or a person assigned to the task by your partner. Although it is unlikely that you would be followed all the time, the knowledge that you may be followed at any time creates the same sense of being under surveillance.

> *Lizzie was contacted by a person she knew from high school. She phoned Lizzie out of the blue. She hadn't seen this person since she left school, and they wanted to catch up with her for a drink. Lizzie felt really anxious. She knew that her abusive partner would disapprove. Further, she knew that no matter where she went or for how long, he would know where she was and what she was doing. She knew she would suffer the consequences of catching up with her friend, disobeying his wishes, and catching up with her without telling him. Not only that, Lizzie was anxious to end the phone call. She knew her partner would want to know who she had spoken to and why. She knew he would be furious.*

How does this affect you?

When you are under surveillance and aware that your behaviour, even normal behaviour, can be used against you at any time, you are likely to feel self-conscious about everything you do. This can make you feel very anxious.

This level of monitoring can make you feel controlled and trapped. You cannot freely decide what you want to do with your day because you have to consider the consequences of what might happen should your partner be aware of your movements. This is true even when you are not doing anything that would be deemed to be problematic by anyone else. It deprives you of a sense of privacy and autonomy, that is, your ability to make choices for yourself.

When you are potentially under surveillance at any time, seeking help regarding your situation is very difficult. If you approach someone who can help you, you risk being found out, putting you and the person you reached out to at risk.

Economic/financial abuse

What is it?

Although it is not unusual for a couple to combine their finances, it is usual for both partners to have a say in how their money is managed and both parties have access to that money. As a form of abuse, the abusive partner controls all money management and distribution. Often, you would be provided with insufficient funds to run the household or engage in self-care despite the abusive partner expecting you to meet impossible standards in these areas.

Further, your abusive partner can make you answerable for every cent you spend. This may involve you providing receipts for every purchase or having sessions when they go through bank statements, with you having to give descriptions of every withdrawal.

> *When discussing how things had been during her relationship with her abusive partner, Jessica related how she struggled to stretch the money her partner gave her to cover what she needed. She had to make the money stretch to feed him and the children, but it was rarely sufficient. As a result, she would skip meals herself to ensure the rest of the family was fed. There was never any money to buy herself clothes or other necessities, and she rarely had the funds to purchase female sanitary products. Asking her partner for more money caused him to become angry, and she would be punished for what he saw as her inability to budget. Trying to manage the small amount of money she was given caused her to feel despair. The struggle was endless. In contrast, her abusive partner would spend money on himself and would indulge the children with expensive toys.*

How does this affect you?

Being concerned about money, even at the best of times, can make you anxious and worried. If you add in the fact that you are also answerable to an abusive partner about your management of money, that anxiety must increase.

Being unable to support your self-care financially can be humiliating as well as anxiety-provoking. Whether or not you can meet your own basic needs is entirely in your abusive partner's control. It is a demeaning action on the part of your abusive partner to put you in a position where you have to be concerned about personal hygiene and care. The degrading nature of this form of abuse can change how you view yourself and your sense of self-worth.

It is problematic for you to try to balance what is expected of you (e.g., provision of physical care for your abusive partner, such as preparation of meals) with your limited means to do so. It is likely to create intense feelings of anxiety when your limited financial means of providing the care is likely to trigger an abusive response in your partner.

The power imbalance in a relationship where one person has all of the control of financial matters and the other person has none is apparent. The lack of power in a relationship causes you to change how you view yourself. It can cause you to have a diminished sense of self-efficacy, which is your belief in your ability to do what you set out to do. Your inability to control your finances is likely to impact your belief in your capacity to care for your needs in other regards because your self-efficacy has been affected.

There are numerous other ways that abuse can manifest. The experience of abuse forms a complex pattern determined by the relationship dynamic. Each one of these types of abuse is problematic and, on the surface, seems to indicate a need to step away from the relationship. However, this complex pattern's features make walking away from the relationship difficult.

The cycle of abuse

A good way of understanding the pattern of abuse in your relationship is to consider a four-stage cycle of abuse. This describes an episode of abuse in terms of what happens before the abuse, at the time of the abuse, and in the aftermath of the abuse. By examining abuse in this way, you can begin to see how you became entangled in this type of relationship.

The four stages of the abuse cycle

There are four main stages of an episode of abuse.

Tension

Initially, there will be a build-up of tension. In an abusive relationship, it does not require that anything stressful has occurred. Instead, it is a pattern of tension increase that is determined by the psychological state of the abusive partner.

Incident

After some time, when tension increases, which can be brief or prolonged, an abusive episode occurs. This is like the climax of this build-up of tension that precedes it. It is like all the tension boils over, and there seems to be no way to avoid it or hold it back.

Reconciliation

The process of reconciliation signifies the end of the abusive episode. Although often an emotionally fraught time, it can be perceived as reassuring because you know that the abusive episode is over. The reconciliation can be characterised by apologies and reassurances that tend to make you feel better after an abusive episode, even if your experience tells you the reassurances of no further abuse are false.

Calm

After the reconciliation, you enter a period of relative calm. This is the rewarding part of the cycle, as a period of calm in an otherwise volatile relationship provides the greatest peace.

What is the impact of this cycle of abuse?

There is an important feature of this cycle of abuse that has an impact on the likelihood of you learning to tolerate abusive episodes in your relationship. If the abusive episode occurred in isolation from other events, each episode would be intolerable because they would be entirely unpredictable, and you would feel threatened all the time. However, abusive episodes do not occur separately from what precedes them or comes after them.

The feature that has the most significant influence on your ability to tolerate abusive episodes is what happens afterwards. The rewarding nature of that period of calm means that you will put up with an abusive episode because you know that a better time is coming. You know that the abuse will end and, even more importantly, it will be followed by the most rewarding time. As that period of calm following the reconciliation period is better than any other time in the relationship, it becomes desirable to have that peace and calm. As a result, you will put up with unhappy times to achieve the happiest times in your relationship.

This process can influence why you stay in a relationship that is not a healthy one for you. Let's consider why you stayed in the relationship for as long as you did.

Why did I stay?

People who have not been in an abusive relationship assume that it is a simple matter to decide to leave and then end the relationship. You have likely heard negative comments about people who do not leave a relationship despite being abused. These comments are typically made by people with no personal experience of the matter. Even if well-intentioned, these comments usually are ill-informed and do not consider the multitude of influences on a person in this situation. There are complex reasons people may not simply walk away.

A complicated issue

It is not unusual that after the end of an abusive relationship, you will spend some time trying to work out why you stayed as long as you did despite the ongoing abuse. The issue is complicated, and it is unlikely that there is a single reason why the relationship continued. It is also unlikely that the reasons for staying in a relationship for one person are the same as why other people stay.

Whatever the reasons, none of them will seem good enough to explain why you did not leave the relationship as soon as the abuse started. Nevertheless, it is worth considering some of the reasons people give for staying in an abusive relationship despite it being unhealthy.

I was too scared to leave

Often, at the beginning of a new relationship, things seem wonderful. This is also true of abusive relationships. By the time you realise that you would be better off out of the relationship, it may be too late. By then, the perpetrator of the abuse may have made threats about what would happen if you ever left. You can come to believe that there would be nowhere to go or hide that would protect you from the perpetrator.

This fear can result from the perpetrator's work to create a persona of omnipotence and omnipresence. That is, they will convince you that they have the power to cause you harm no matter what protections you have put in place and that there is no institution, such as the courts or police, that can override that power. Further, they can convince you that they have a presence, either in person or through family or associates, that will place you under surveillance no matter where you go.

It is the case that your fear about leaving may not be or may not only be about the threat to you that the perpetrator represents. You may fear what would happen to others you care about, such as your family or friends. A threat to a vulnerable family member may act as a barrier to you seeing a way to separate from the perpetrator of the abuse successfully.

Another reason you may be too scared to leave is the threats made about the care of your children. The abuser may make threats that you will have your children taken from you and that they will remain living with the abuser. He may claim that you will not see your children again. This can feel very threatening for a person whose confidence and belief in themselves have been undermined by the process of extended abuse.

> *Evelyn's ex-partner had made repeated threats throughout their relationship. He had threatened to harm their children. He had threatened to kill Evelyn. He had threatened to harm her dog. He had threatened to go to child protective services and report her for physically harming the children. Whenever he was unhappy, he made these types of threats. He had also said that he would be the one who decided when the relationship ended, and if she tried to leave him, he would carry out these threats. Evelyn felt at the time that she couldn't take the risk of these things happening should she leave her partner.*

He said he would kill himself if I left

The fear you experienced at the thought of leaving the relationship may not only have been related to your safety or the safety of your family and friends. It also may have been linked to your fear that the abuser would take his own life.

These threats of the abuser taking his own life if you do not do as he demands are reasonably common. In most instances, they represent a form of emotional blackmail and do not reflect a genuine intention to suicide. These threats rely on you feeling guilty at the thought of another person taking their life because of an action or failure to act on your part.

Of course, what we know about suicide threats as a form of emotional blackmail does not rule out the possibility that a person will follow through with the threat. When these suicides occur, they tend to be impulsive. Typically, very little planning is involved, and they are more likely to happen in the heat of the moment as emotions escalate in intensity.

This can be true, even in the context of repeated threats. As a person talks more about suicide, it becomes easier to consider ending one's own life. Then, when there has been an escalation in conflict or stress, a person may act impulsively.

Of course, none of this makes you responsible for the actions taken by another person. You cannot live your life in a way that is aimed at preventing another person from suiciding. It is not even possible to do so. If you are concerned, you would be better off asking the police to do a welfare check. They are in a much better position to obtain assistance for the suicidal individual than are you.

> *Adalee learned early on in her relationship not to discuss her unhappiness or suggest she wanted to leave. Her attempts to have a conversation about the state of their relationship would result in her partner threatening to kill himself. Indeed, any comment at all about her dissatisfaction with the relationship would result in escalating threats of self-harm that were emotionally fraught, exhausting and frightening. Despite times when she genuinely wanted to leave the relationship, she did not want anything bad to happen to her partner. Before long, Adalee learned it was better to keep her concerns to herself. She resigned herself to the notion that she would be trapped in the relationship forever.*

But I loved him…

Many people say they did not leave the abusive relationship because they loved their partner. Without questioning that depth of feeling, it must be considered that loving feelings in a relationship that is associated with such negative and threatening experiences are complicated ones. For those uninvolved, it might be hard to see how you can love someone who deliberately causes you harm.

The feelings of love can be confused by a combination of other feelings and relationship processes. When we are in a relationship, we form an attachment to that person. The bond that develops is an emotional one that is built on three elements that are warmth (the expression of warm feelings towards each other), empathic involvement (being engaged with the person and involved in their life) and continuity of contact (regular contact and communication). This bond is difficult to break, even if your partner does terrible things. However, after the relationship is over, this attachment will end because those three elements are no longer present.

Loving feelings can be confused with feelings of dependence. Feeling like you cannot live without your partner is not the same thing as an intense feeling of love. Feelings of dependence relate to a belief that you need to rely on your partner and cannot cope without that person. However, in the case of abusive romantic relationships, these feelings can go beyond feelings of dependence and reach a state of anxious dependency.

Anxious dependency refers to feelings of fear at the thought of losing the relationship with the person on whom you are dependent. To stop the feelings of fear at the thought of the relationship ending, you might tolerate more abusive behaviour than you would if that fear did not exist.

Anxious dependency is often encouraged by the perpetrator of abuse. They might tell you that you cannot cope without them, that you would never cope alone, and that no other person would ever want you. These tactics are used to tie you to the abuser and to reduce the chance that you will leave.

One issue that needs to be considered is how loving feelings towards an abusive partner can be misinterpreted by the person experiencing those feelings. Part of the problem with misinterpreting feelings of love comes from the 'roller coaster ride' of emotions that are experienced as a result of the changing behaviours of the abuser.

If the abuser mistreated you all of the time and from the outset, you would not have stayed in the relationship. Of course, at the start of the relationship, a partner who turns out to be abusive will typically treat you well. You enter into the relationship believing that the good treatment you are receiving will continue. Then the abuse begins, sometimes building up in intensity over time or sometimes surprising you by its intensity from the first attack on you. This is often followed by a period when the abuser claims to be regretful and will act in a repentant way. This usually entails a period when the abuser is being nice to you.

In comparison to the dreadful experience of the abuse, those periods between the abusive episodes seem lovely. However, typically, they are not wonderful times as perceived by people who are not abused. We would argue that these periods of relative calm are the absolute minimum you should expect in a loving relationship with your partner. The trouble is that you tend to misinterpret these experiences as more positive than they are by other standards, and these misinterpretations cause a strengthening of loving feelings towards your partner that, in a sense, have been falsely generated.

> *When things were bad in Iris' relationship with her former partner, they were terrible. His behaviour was unpredictable, volatile, and, Iris believed, dangerous. She knew that his behaviour was having a terrible impact on her. At times, his behaviour was so out of control that she feared he would kill her. At those times, all Iris wanted to do was escape him. However, there were times when her former partner would behave lovingly. Indeed, there were lots of those times. Iris would be reminded of why she fell in love with him, and she would find herself feeling very protective towards him, understanding that he had significant problems. She wanted to help him. She would defend him to her friends when they questioned her about his behaviour. At those times, when he was at his most loving, she could not imagine leaving her ex-partner. She loved him.*

The abuser's expressions of regret and promises of change

It is not unusual for an abusive partner to promise to change, especially immediately after an abusive episode. At these times, the abuser will seem genuinely regretful and will treat you in a loving way. As a result, you end up feeling sorry for the abuser despite this being undeserved, and you give them another chance.

> *When describing what had happened to her in the relationship with her ex-partner, Daisy gave an account of an occasion when she was cowering in the corner while her ex-partner had repeatedly punched her. She said she had felt her eye and lip swelling. She said she remembered him shouting and foaming at the mouth because he was so angry. She remembered begging him to stop. But, the next morning, he was very remorseful, she recounted. He pleaded with her to forgive him, and he promised he would get help. He promised he would never become so out of control again. He seemed so genuine. Daisy recalled a feeling of hope that sprang up inside her. She believed he intended to keep his word and do something about his problems. Despite him never seeking help, Daisy still felt that his remorse was genuine and his intentions were good. After all, things did improve for a while.*

There were children involved

You may choose to stay in an abusive relationship because there are children involved. You may believe that it is not fair to the children to remove them from their father. It is most often the case that the children will love their father, and moving them away from their father seems unreasonable. Of course, arguments can be made about why it is an entirely reasonable course of action.

You may believe, somewhat mistakenly, that your abusive partner would never hurt the children. You may see him as a good father. This would make it difficult for you to decide to take the children away from their other parent. However, good arguments can be made that the home of an abusive person is an unsafe environment for children.

Also, you may have found it difficult to leave with children for pragmatic reasons. A need to provide a stable home for children and a need to keep them fed and clothed may have encouraged you to stay in an abusive relationship for longer than you would have done had you only had your own needs to consider.

> *Gianna had children with her former partner. He had been abusive towards her throughout much of their relationship. Gianna took comfort in the fact that her partner's abuse was directed at her and not at the children. Indeed, she often described her partner as a good father who loved and cared for the children. This was even though their father's behaviour impacted the children. He often had explosive episodes when the children were present, and he had threatened Gianna with a knife when the children were in the room. Gianna had struggled to leave the relationship because she did not want to deprive the children of their father. She knew she could not leave them in their father's care without her protection. When she thought about leaving, she worried that, in her absence, her partner would turn his angry behaviour towards the children.*

Loss of sense of self-efficacy and self-confidence

Self-confidence refers to your belief in yourself and your view of your abilities. Self-efficacy refers to your belief in your capacity to do what you set out to do. Both need to be healthy to successfully navigate life's demands. They allow you to believe you have the skills to deal with life problems and to follow through and resolve the problems you face.

An abusive relationship will undermine your self-confidence and self-efficacy, making it difficult for you to leave a relationship that is unhealthy for you. You struggle to believe that you would be able to look after yourself if you left the relationship.

Problems with self-efficacy and self-confidence can occur because of the messages either directly given to you by an abusive partner or from the implied messages you receive because of the abuse. Direct messages might be comments made by the abusive partner, such as telling you how stupid you are and how you cannot do anything right. Indirect messages might come in the form of an association between perceived wrongdoing (e.g., not having a meal cooked on time) and an episode of abuse where you end up criticising yourself.

What happens is that you then take on board these messages. You come to believe what your abusive partner is telling you, either through words or actions. You feel stupid. You think that you cannot do anything without making a mistake. You certainly do not feel like you could face the demands of life alone.

> *Isla had thought often about leaving the relationship with her abusive partner. She knew what was happening to her was bad for her. She worried that she would come to serious harm. She even worried that someone would report the abuse and her partner would end up in prison. She thought that nothing good could come out of continuing the relationship. However, whenever she seriously thought about leaving, Isla was overwhelmed by all the difficulties and challenges she would face in doing so. She couldn't imagine coping with finding somewhere else to live. She was overwhelmed at the thought of getting her possessions out of their joint property. She couldn't imagine working on a property settlement with regard to the house they jointly owned. The list of challenges seemed to be endless. Isla thought she couldn't do any of these things. Isla thought maybe her partner was right that she was hopeless and couldn't do anything. Perhaps he had a point.*

Low sense of self-worth

Another consequence of an abusive relationship is that you can develop a low sense of self-worth. Self-worth refers to a view you have of yourself that you are good enough and worthy of being held in high regard by others. Whereas self-esteem relies on external indicators of achievement (e.g., I feel good because I got a promotion at work), self-worth is an internal view you have of yourself and your value as a person (e.g., no one would love me if they knew how useless I am).

People with low self-worth always critically evaluate themselves, thinking they are not doing a good enough job. They focus on their mistakes, failures, and the things they did not do but maybe should have done. In relationships, people with low self-worth will go out of their way to please their partner and are more likely to tolerate neglect and abuse than people with healthier levels of self-worth.

> *Charlotte had been told often enough by her abusive partner that she was worthless. She was inclined to believe that was true. Indeed, she never seemed to be able to do anything right, as nothing she did pleased her partner... no matter how hard she tried. Charlotte sometimes thought about leaving the relationship, and that gave her a moment of hope. However, she would then think that no one else would want to be in a relationship with someone as useless as her, and she couldn't bear the thought of a lifetime alone. Those hopeful thoughts of leaving were then overridden by a belief that she was better off having someone in her life than no one, even if her partner treated her badly. After all, she couldn't expect the happiness other people had because she didn't deserve it.*

Lack of social support

A perceived lack of social support can contribute to the reason why people do not feel they can leave an abusive relationship. Firstly, you might believe you have no one to turn to for support. This may be the result of the social isolation that was created by the limits placed on you by your abusive partner. As previously described, abusive partners tend to isolate their partners from the significant people in their lives because they do not want others to influence their partners. If that separation from the important people in your life has been occurring over a lengthy period, you may not feel comfortable reaching out to people whose relationships with you have diminished.

You may not have wanted to reach out to the people who used to support you, fearing they would reject your request for help. There may be a history of your family and friends encouraging you to leave the relationship, being aware of the abuse you were experiencing. You may simply believe these people have abandoned you because of your reluctance to take their advice. Alternatively, you may feel that your family and friends would not choose to support you because of their resentment that you have abandoned them when you were forced to withdraw at your partner's insistence.

You may have been reluctant to seek help from family and friends to leave the abusive relationship because you did not wish to disclose the abuse and involve others in the matter. You may have a genuine concern for the well-being of others, believing that by involving them, you would draw the attention of the abuser, putting them at risk. Alternatively, you simply may be embarrassed.

> *Bobbi was miserable. For a long time, she had put up with the abuse her partner directed towards her. Earlier in the relationship, Bobbi had thought that things might improve, but over time, she had realised that wasn't going to happen. However, the thought of actually leaving the relationship made her feel overwhelmed and lonely. Despite previously having close relationships with her family, Bobbi had not had any contact with them for some time. Her partner had disliked her having contact with her family, and it hadn't been worth the arguments to push the point with him. Bobbi also felt she had no friends. Her good friends had disappeared over time because her partner had hated them and reacted poorly if she had tried to see them. So, Bobbi felt isolated and alone. She had no one she thought would help her leave, and she wasn't sure she could do it alone.*

As can be seen, there are complex reasons for persevering with an abusive relationship. These reasons may be ones that other people do not fully understand. There is one other aspect of abusive relationships that can influence whether you have the courage to leave. This is a process engaged in by the abuser to make you feel responsible for the difficulties you experience and the failure of the relationship.

The issue of gaslighting

One important issue that needs to be discussed about the impact of abuse on you and how you may need to learn to move forward is 'gaslighting'. According to the American Psychological Association, gaslighting refers to the manipulation of another person into 'doubting their own perceptions, experiences or understanding of events".

Types of gaslighting

There are four types of gaslighting. Each type has similarities with other types. Namely, they all reflect dishonesty in the effort to deny your experiences as genuine and that you are identified as the person with the problem rather than the abuser.

Outright lying

If you question a gaslighting abuser, they will lie. These lies are told with boldness and arrogance, with the goal of making you believe your concerns are unfounded and unwarranted. The lies are frequent and unrelenting. Gaslighting abusers will lie even when the lie is pointless and unnecessary.

> *Michelle had strong suspicions that her partner was cheating on her. Then, two of her friends approached her and told her they had seen him with another woman being openly affectionate. She then saw her partner with this other woman. Michelle raised the issue with her partner. He told her that there was no other woman in his life, and it was not true that he had been openly affectionate with anyone. He told Michelle she had not seen him with another woman. He told Michelle that her friends had lied to hurt him. He said they were jealous of him and wanted to destroy him. He asked Michelle if she would allow their jealousy and dishonesty to destroy their relationship. He asked her if she was going to let these people win. He called her a fool for believing them.*

All this lying does is create mistrust in the relationship. An abuser who gaslights should not be trusted based on what they say but on their behaviour. You should pay attention to what they do but not necessarily what they say.

This type of lying is a form of manipulation. It serves to isolate you from both the truth and from others who may support you. By the abuser insisting they are not at fault and the person who conveyed information to you about the abuser is wrong, you are less likely to trust your family member or friend. The abusive partner's insistence that they are telling the truth, even in the face of evidence to the contrary, encourages you to believe them. You can then feel guilty for challenging or questioning the abuser.

Manipulation of reality

This is where your experiences and perceptions are challenged by the abuser in terms of their reality. If what you think and experience is constantly challenged, you are likely to start to doubt yourself with regard to your recollections and your judgment. In the longer term, this process can have a detrimental effect on your mental health. Even if you have evidence to prove your version of events is correct, you can still come to doubt yourself and accept the gaslighting abuser's perspective. This results in you not trusting yourself to know what is accurate and inaccurate.

> *Olivia had been looking forward to her sister's wedding. It was in another state, but her partner had agreed that they could afford the airfare, and she would be attending. Olivia had made arrangements to stay at a cousin's home. However, when Olivia mentioned having to book her flight, her partner asked her what she was talking about. He claimed he had never agreed that she could go and said he was unprepared to pay for the airfares. He told her she would have to undo the arrangements she had made. When Olivia objected, he said the mix-up was all Olivia's fault. He said this was a problem that happened over and over again. He claimed that Olivia would 'get the wrong end of the stick' and would assume he had said things he would never have said. He complained that Olivia never remembered things correctly. He said it wasn't his fault she would have to cancel her plans as she shouldn't have made them in the first place.*

If they believe the relationship is under threat, a gaslighting abuser may swap their approach for a period of time and agree with your version of events. They typically do this for as long as is necessary to re-establish the strength of the relationship. The effect of this switching from cold to warm behaviour can be that you begin to question whether your concerns are warranted and conclude that the state of the relationship might not be as bad as you thought.

Scapegoating

Scapegoating occurs when the gaslighting abuser holds you responsible for things they have done. The goal is to shift responsibility for wrongdoing from themselves to you in an effort to justify their behaviour. The unrelenting criticisms result in you, the scapegoat, taking on the burden of responsibility for the poor behaviour of the gaslighter. When you are put in a position of having to defend yourself for something you have not done, it is easy to be distracted from the real causes of the problem and the actual perpetrator of the wrongdoing.

> *Amanda was worried. Her partner was becoming increasingly angry. He had failed to renew the car registration, and Amanda had been stopped by the police and fined for driving an unregistered vehicle. Amanda had reminded him the registration was due to be renewed. Her partner was the person who had complete control of the finances in the home, and he always paid the bills. When her partner said he was angry with Amanda about the registration not being paid, she pointed out that he was the person who paid the bills and was in charge of the purse strings. He accused Amanda of always trying to twist things around so that it seemed like his fault when she was actually the one to blame. He kept getting angrier and louder. When she apologised and asked him not to be angry with her, he blamed Amanda for his anger. If she hadn't got them into this mess, he told her, he would not have had to become angry.*

This type of gaslighting effectively prevents good communication in a relationship. You are the person who has to constantly defend your integrity and change to improve yourself despite not being responsible for the problems that suggest the need for change. In contrast, the actual perpetrator of the wrongdoing does not need to change and can adopt the stance of a long-suffering victim of your poor treatment. You feel shame, and the gaslighting abuser gets off scot-free.

Coercion

There is a range of behaviours that can be considered coercive in nature. These can range from trying to 'sweet talk' you into doing what the abuser wants, through to applying undue pressure on you in an emotionally or verbally manipulative way to do what the abuser wants, to violent and overtly bullying behaviour.

> *Brianna's partner was insisting he take photographs of her engaging in sexual behaviours that she did not feel comfortable doing in any case. Not only did she feel embarrassed about having to engage in the sexual behaviours he was demanding, but she also did not trust what he intended to do with the images. She was not convinced he would not post them online or show them to his friends. When she begged him not to insist, her partner started by saying that she would do what he wanted if she loved him, so her refusal must mean she didn't love him. When she was still reluctant, he said she was being overly sensitive. He called her prudish and said other women would jump at the chance to do what he was asking. He then accused her of deliberately withholding love and affection and said it was unfair of her to do this, given how much he did for her. He kept up his demands until Brianna agreed to do as he wished. Her worry about what he was going to do with the images did not go away.*

Coercive control aims to keep the gaslighting abuser in charge, to get you to do what the abuser wants, and to make you feel dependent on the abuser for decision-making. A previously self-sufficient person in charge of decisions in their lives can still be vulnerable to this manipulative process.

What should I be looking for?

If you are being gaslighted, there are common things said by abusers that should ring alarm bells for you. Below are some examples with explanations of why such statements are problematic. Tick the ones you have heard said to you.

Table 1: Examples of gaslighting statements and how they affect you.

	Examples of gaslighting statements
	"What are you complaining about? I only did what I did because I was trying to help you." Statements like this challenge your view that you are justified in feeling angry about the abuser's behaviour. They aim to make you feel guilty about feeling angry. You begin to doubt the validity of your feelings. Self-doubt creeps in, and you find yourself apologising for your emotional reaction to the abuser's behaviour.
	"I don't know what you are talking about. That's not how it happened." In sometimes obvious and sometimes subtle ways, a gaslighting abuser will change the story of an event or their behaviour to suit their purposes. They will then make you believe that you are the one who is mistaken in recalling what happened. By doing this, the abuser has control over your 'reality'.
	"You are crazy." By blatantly denying your reality and identifying you as crazy for believing what you do, the gaslighting abuser wants to make you doubt yourself. Over time, this reduces your self-confidence and increases your anxiety. You start to question your interpretation of events, and the chances you will not challenge the abuser are increased.

	"Carrying on like this, it's no wonder you don't have any friends." An abuser will try to isolate you from your family and friends. They will then try to devalue you and make you feel bad about yourself for having no friends, a situation the abuser created. An abuser may even go so far as to talk to people in your life about your poor attitude, unacceptable treatment of the abuser and lack of commitment to the relationship in an effort to ensure the important people in your life are unsupportive of you. To do this, they paint themselves as the victim of your uncaring attitude and behaviour.
	"This is all your fault." Gaslighting abusers will refuse to accept blame and pass the blame onto you when it suits them to do so… which is often. Refusing to accept responsibility and blaming you for the situation creates feelings of confusion. You doubt your understanding of what is happening. When this occurs, the abuser has been successful in ridding themselves of the burden of responsibility and making you believe you have done wrong.
	"What does it matter? This isn't important." By minimising the importance of your concerns, the gaslighting abuser is trying to devalue you. They create a situation where you begin to question your own understanding of the event that has worried you. With the abuser dismissing the importance of your concern, you are likely to reach a conclusion that your reaction is excessive and unnecessary, thus distorting your sense of reality.
	"You've got it wrong. That's not what I meant." When challenged by you about a hurtful comment they made to you, a gaslighting abuser will either deny they said it or try to change the meaning of what they said. When this is done often enough, you can start to question your interpretation of what was said. This causes you to doubt yourself despite you probably being accurate in your interpretation of the intention of the comment.
	"I don't know what you are going on about. It's not that big of a deal." By diminishing the importance of your reaction to something the gaslighting abuser has said or done, the abuser is devaluing you. They try to make you feel that you have overreacted and you are the one at fault.

	"You're overreacting. You're too sensitive." In an effort to devalue you, gaslighting abusers will challenge you in terms of the intensity of your feelings, making you feel like you have been wrong to have a strong response to inappropriate behaviour on the abuser's part. Doing this increases your self-doubt and diminishes your self-worth.
	"What are you going on about? It was only a joke." Telling you that what was said was 'only a joke' is a way for a gaslighting abuser to deliver a cutting 'put-down'. By doing this, the abuser is forcing you to question your ability to distinguish between fact and fiction. It undermines your confidence in your ability to know what you are feeling is the case.
	"Stop over-analysing it." In an effort to undermine your interpretation of events relating to their behaviour, a gaslighting abuser will accuse you of holding the view you do only because you are overthinking the problem. This belittling action causes you to feel less certain about your understanding of what you have experienced.
	"Nothing is going on. You are just paranoid." Rather than admit to wrongdoing, a gaslighting abuser will accuse you of being overly suspicious. In this way, they are encouraging you to believe you have made a mistake in accusing them of doing the wrong thing. You start to question the evidence on which you have based your view and, therefore, doubt yourself.
	"That didn't happen. You're just making it up." Rather than accept they have done the wrong thing, a gaslighting abuser may simply accuse you of lying when you raise an issue about their behaviour. Attempts on your part to defend yourself will cause the abuser to forcefully increase the strength of their accusation that you have fabricated the problem. This can lead to intense distress on your part that cannot be expressed easily.
	"You're just overreacting." Being told you are overreacting to something that is concerning for you in relation to your partner's behaviour is just another way of challenging the validity of your reactions.

	"I really don't know what you want me to say." When you are asking for an explanation for a partner's poor behaviour, a response of feigned confusion conveys a message that there is not anything they could say that would be acceptable to you. This transfers the responsibility for explaining the problem from the abuser to you, the person who asked for the explanation in the first place.
	"Everyone else is on my side and agrees with me." No matter how unlikely such a statement is, claiming that everyone agrees with the abuser and thus disagrees with you makes you feel everyone is against you. Gaslighting abusers make these sorts of statements to encourage you to think you are wrong and to back down and not further challenge the abuser.
	"I didn't do anything wrong. How dare you say I did." It is a more severe version of accusing you of being wrong. It makes you the target of the accusation of wrongdoing. Many people who are put in this situation end up apologising despite them not engaging in the inappropriate behaviour, partly to end the accusations but also because they come to believe they might be to blame for getting the situation wrong.
	"It's not fair. I'm never allowed to let you know how I am feeling." In response to any expression by you about your concerns about their volatile behaviour, the gaslighting abuser turns the situation around and blames you for being insensitive to their needs. The goal is to move attention away from their own poor behaviour and make you feel bad.
	"Here you go again, blowing things out of proportion, just like you always do." Statements such as this cause you to question your judgment. However, making claims that you 'always' do something is bound to be an exaggeration and does not accurately reflect the situation.
	"Let's not talk about it right now." By insisting that a discussion be postponed, the gaslighting abuser is attempting to divert your focus with the hope that the issue that triggered the discussion is not discussed again. You never get the chance to express your concerns or talk about how you feel about a matter.

	"You don't have a clue." Telling you that you have no idea what you are talking about is a way of shutting down a discussion. A gaslighting abuser is more likely to use such a tactic if they do not like the way the conversation is going and they are struggling to find other ways of deflecting attention away from their own poor behaviour.
	"Who do you think they are going to believe, you or me?" The gaslighting abuser may ask such a question so that you doubt the degree of support you would receive for your perspective and to cause you to doubt your perspective of the abuser being the wrongdoer. However, it cannot be ruled out that the abuser actually believes that they would be perceived to be the person in the superior position, no matter how unlikely that would be the case.
	"You're going on about me, but you're not perfect, either." By pointing out your faults, the gaslighting abuser is attempting to deflect attention away from the actual topic of discussion, that is their behaviour. You then are put into a position where you either have to defend yourself or accept that you have no right to raise a complaint about your partner's behaviour.
	"Let's just forgive and forget and move on." The goal of the gaslighting abuser is to shut down the discussion. However, it also puts the burden of responsibility on you to be the one who lets go of an issue that concerns you without the abuser having to do anything.
	"Not this again. You are always going over the past." No gaslighting abuser wants to revisit the past. In fact, they would rather rewrite the past to cast themselves as the hero and reinterpret their role in events that you recall as abusive. If done in the way the abuser wants, you will come away feeling like you are the one causing the problem.
	"After all that I've done for you, is this how you treat me?" The goal here is to divert attention from the poor behaviour of the gaslighting abuser and onto you. In doing this, the abuser is trying to create a situation where you feel guilty and are likely to back off from any challenge in relation to the abuser's behaviour.
	"We have been over this already. I can't believe you don't remember." Here, the gaslighting abuser is trying to rewrite history and pretend that the matter has been resolved. It is a strategy used by the abuser to make you question your memory.

	"Here we go again. You always have to be right." Despite the fact that it is the gaslighting abuser who always has to be right, they try to make out this is a shortcoming you possess. In doing so, they are encouraging you to form the view that you are the one being unreasonable.
	"There is something wrong with you. You need to get some help." In an effort to invalidate what you are thinking and feeling and to move the attention away from their actions and onto your mental health, the gaslighting abuser will try to make you feel like 'normal' people would not think the way you do.
	"What an imagination!" This statement has the same effect as telling you that you are making things up. It is a deflection technique used by the gaslighting abuser to make you question your interpretation of events.
	"You always think you're so smart." Such a statement is designed to convey the opposite, that you are not smart and you are mistaken about the views you are holding. This tactic is aimed at devaluing you and causing you to back down from questioning the actions of the abuser.
	"I don't know what you are talking about. You're not making sense." The purpose here is to make you feel uncertain about your ability to convey your concerns. However, the underlying goal is to take the focus away from your concerns and place it on your capacity to communicate what you are trying to say.
	"What are you doing? You are just trying to confuse me." Gaslighting actions and comments are designed to confuse you and distract you from what the gaslighting abuser is trying to do. A claim that you are trying to confuse them typically has no basis.
	"Get your facts straight." This is another way of getting you to question yourself. By simply denying that what you are saying is the truth, the gaslighting abuser is attempting to deflect attention away from their own problematic behaviour.

	"You never said that." / "I never said that." The goal here is to get you to doubt your memory of events. Such tactics try to make you feel like you do not have a grip on your recall or your sanity.

Checklist version available at elemen.com.au

As you can see, there are many ways in which an abusive partner can gaslight you. All are dishonest representations of what actually happened, and all are designed to throw you off balance.

Indicators of gaslighting and the effects on you

Before moving on, let's consider whether you have been on the receiving end of gaslighting by your abusive partner and whether it has affected your mental health.

	Indicators of gaslighting and the effects on you
	Have you been having trouble making decisions, even simple ones?
	Have you often made excuses to your family and friends about your partner's behaviour?
	Are you constantly having to second-guess yourself?
	Have you blamed yourself for your partner treating you badly?
	Have you tried to convince yourself that your partner's poor behaviour is not really that bad?
	Have you had to walk on eggshells around your partner?
	Have you questioned yourself about whether you are too sensitive?
	Have things your partner said caused you to question the validity of your thoughts, feelings, judgments, and observations?
	Did you feel lonely and trapped in your relationship with your partner?
	Have you doubted your own memory and your sanity?

	Have you ever kept quiet with your partner when you felt you should have spoken up about what you believed or thought?
	Have you felt on edge much of the time and threatened?
	Have you felt your partner might be correct when he accused you of being stupid or crazy?
	Have you ever felt that you could not do anything right and been disappointed in who you turned out to be?
	Did you spend a lot of time apologising for your actions even though apologising was not necessary?

Checklist available at elemen.com.au

Gaslighting can have a profound and ongoing effect on how you view yourself and how you trust your own feelings, thoughts and memories. These effects then need to be undone. We will consider ways to challenge the effects later in this workbook.

My reaction to the end of the relationship

Here, we need to consider briefly your reaction to the end of the relationship. Dealing with the aftermath can be as difficult as dealing with the relationship while you are in it.

The abuser ended the relationship

When it is the abuser who ended the relationship, you are faced with the challenge of dealing with the fact that you have lost something that you once thought you could not cope without. Often, you are ill-prepared to deal with the abrupt end of the relationship. You have had no time to consider this happening and you are not in your best frame of mind to cope with the challenges associated with a relationship ending. When you are at your lowest ebb, you must deal with additional problems.

Of course, the fact that your abusive partner ended the relationship does not mean that he will move on and leave you to recover. He can still continue to expect to have control over you and what you do. He can still seek to torment you because he believes it is his right to do so. This can create additional problems for you at a time when you are trying to get your life back on track.

You ended the relationship

Even if it is the case that you ended the relationship, you can still face a period of difficult adjustment. You need to work on undoing the psychological damage done to you. The challenge of moving forward can be made more difficult because you have to work on reaching a point where you feel able to retake charge of your life.

You also have additional worries about the threats that may have been made to you in anticipation of you ending the relationship. You have a need to protect yourself in case your abusive former partner follows through with those threats. Just as may occur when the abuser ends the relationship, your former partner may not leave you alone to get on with your life. His inability to accept your decision may cause him to act in ways that make your adjustment more challenging.

Grief and disenfranchised grief

Although your relationship with your abusive ex-partner was a difficult one, it is worth taking a moment to consider that you may react to the loss of that relationship with feelings of grief.

What is grief?

Grief is a universally experienced emotional reaction to loss or perceived loss. It can also be experienced in relation to expected loss (anticipatory grief) or in situations where you or others might not recognise that grief is warranted (disenfranchised grief). Grief is experienced in relation to the loss of someone or something important to you. For example, you may grieve the loss of a future you expected to have available to you but did not turn out the way you wanted.

Typically, grief is experienced in stages. Acute grief occurs in the immediate period after a loss. These feelings of grief occur irrespective of the event that triggered it. This type of grief is associated with severe or intense feelings of distress.

In the initial phase of acute grief, you can feel shock and numbness. You feel disengaged from what is happening. This dissociative experience is protective, in a sense, shielding you from the intensity of the emotional reactions to the loss. However, there will come a time when the full strength of your emotional reactions will be felt.

The emotional reactions to the loss you have experienced can be varied and may change over the course of the period of acute grief. Although we typically associate grief with feelings of sadness, grief can also be related to feelings of anger, guilt, anguish, regret or relief, depending on the circumstances of the loss and all the things that came before

These emotional reactions to loss can be painful. In the beginning, they may seem to be always present. However, before long, this changes, and you experience feelings of grief in bursts or waves. These waves of grief tend to be triggered by specific reminders of your loss or things that make you think about the person in the context of better times.

These waves of grief lessen over time, both in terms of their frequency of occurrence and in their strength or intensity. This reduction will allow you to regain a feeling of emotional balance. At this time, your attention will be more focused on events outside of you rather than on your emotional state.

The next phase is what is known as integrated grief. This is experienced after you transition beyond the acute grief stage. To reach a point of integrated grief, it may take you several months or more, or may occur sooner.

There are signs that you have moved to integrated grief. For example, you will be able to think about the person or what you have lost without the overwhelming nature of your earlier emotional responses. You can pick up your life again, returning to work and engaging in activities that give you pleasure.

It is often the case that you can move forward with a better perspective on life, a greater understanding of what is important in life, and a new focus on the things that matter. These positive changes in outlook have been identified to occur after a severe and often traumatic life event or events. These life events act as a catalyst for you to change your outlook on life. It causes you to reprioritise things so that your focus is more on the important issues in your life and less on the more minor things that no longer seem to matter.

For most people, this is the point where you move on with your life, being the new person you have become due to the loss you have experienced. However, for a small number of people, this is more challenging to achieve., For those people, complicated grief is experienced when people struggle to overcome their acute grief phase. The feelings of longing and loss do not abate over time. However, complicated grief is not the typical outcome of a grieving process. Most people transition through to a point where they can experience life in a meaningful way.

Disenfranchised grief

One of the factors that can make grieving more difficult is when the grief you experience is disenfranchised. What does this mean? Disenfranchised grief is when your grief reaction does not fit with society's expectations. Our society has created certain expectations regarding how people grieve and about what they should grieve. When the trigger for your grief or how you are grieving does not fit with those societal expectations, you can feel disenfranchised.

Disenfranchised grief can occur in numerous contexts. Importantly for our discussion here, your grief over a loss that is not death (e.g., the loss of a relationship), your grief for something that did not actually occur (e.g., loss of a future you hoped to have), or grief for the loss of a loved one from your life even though that person abused you and caused you harm are all likely to disenfranchise your grief. In all of these cases, it is hard to obtain the same sympathy and support received by people who are grieving a loss in more societally approved ways or because of experiences society sees as acceptable reasons for grieving.

Indeed, even though this is not true, disenfranchised grief is typically considered to be less important or less significant than more commonly accepted grief. As a result, you can experience disregard for your feelings. As a consequence of this disregard, you can be denied the right to mourn in the usual sense or in the way you would typically choose to mourn.

Of course, disenfranchised grief does not make the grief less real for you. The fact that others do not validate your feelings does not mean they are not legitimate. It may mean that you will need to seek other avenues for expressing your grief or different ways of seeking the help and support you need. Consider the following ways of helping you cope.

Table 2: Ways of coping with disenfranchised grief.

Seek out supportive people who understand what you are experiencing. These might be people who have experienced similar grief, or they may be people who understand what you have lost and how important this loss is to you. They may also be people who have a more thorough understanding of your relationship and appreciate the value to you of aspects of the relationship you have lost.
Create a mourning ritual that is important to you. Rituals are often important in the mourning process. In the absence of other means of expressing your grief, you may keep items that have a sentimental value. You may prepare an album of photographs of important events in your relationship. You might write a farewell letter to your ex-partner without any intention of ever sending it.
Ask for the help you need. Without having to disclose the reasons why you are seeking assistance, you can still ask for help. Let your support network of family and friends know when you need company, need to be distracted by an activity, or need someone to listen to you talk.
Seek professional help. When you need to discuss your grief in a non-judgmental environment, professional help can provide you with that opportunity. Seeking professional help can also assist you to normalise your grief so that you see it is a natural reaction to loss despite the rejection of this by others.

So, you have experienced the abuse and your emotional reaction to it. The effects on you can feel quite profound. What do you do about it now?

What do I need to do now?

So, what do you do now that the relationship has ended? Let's consider what you may need.

We will be making some comments about how to protect yourself and keep yourself safe. We will direct you to information about things you can do for yourself and services you may choose to access.

We will teach you to manage the anxiety you feel. We will provide you with information about how your nervous system functions and give you reasons why your nervous system is in an overly aroused state. This will be followed by introducing you to ways you can control what your nervous system is doing and inviting you to learn to quiet your mind so that you can control your distress.

Following this, we will apply some of these skills to the management of sleep disturbance if you are having trouble with insomnia. We will explain your sleep cycle and provide you with reasons why your sleep is disturbed. We will then introduce some simple strategies for helping you sleep better.

We will then introduce you to the notion of coping and explore your preferred ways of coping with life problems. We will then show you ways to build on your effective coping strategies or build new and better ones.

Attention will then be given to the way you think and how errors in thinking can influence how you feel and how you behave. These errors in thinking can have their foundation in the types of experiences you have had in the abusive relationship and the messages you received from your abusive partner. They are related to how you view the world, how you view your place in the world, and how you view your future. After an abusive relationship, you can view the world as more threatening, yourself as less worthy, and the future as more dangerous and unpredictable than necessary.

When you have learned ways to improve your thinking, you can pay some attention to re-establishing your sense of self and your self-worth. These are particular aspects of you that are often affected by abusive experiences. Indeed, the actions of your abusive partner could have deliberately targeted these areas to undermine you.

We will then focus on rebuilding your self-efficacy, which is your belief that you can achieve what you set out to do. Self-efficacy is often damaged by the messages you have received in your relationship that you are incapable and incompetent.

It can be difficult to understand your rights after being treated in an invalidating, denigrating and demeaning way. We will cover your basic rights that you are entitled to defend.

Then, we will teach you ways to advocate for your rights assertively, cover ways to ask for change and negotiate for a good outcome. This is important after a period of time when your wishes were dismissed or considered secondary to your abusive partner's wishes.

Finally, we will consider ways you can improve the quality of your life. This can help you regain the things in your life that you value the most.

Keep yourself safe

Here, we would like to emphasise the importance of keeping yourself safe. Because the steps you should take are not strictly a psychological issue, rather than cover all the things you need to do, we would like to direct you to a website, yourtoolkit.com, that provides a comprehensive account of what you need to do and the resources available to you in Australia should you need to access them. The information about what you need to do is relevant for people wherever you live. However, if you live in a country other than Australia, look for similar websites that can provide you with information about specific services available to you.

yourtoolkit.com

Consistent with the information contained on this website and to give you an idea of the things you need to consider, we have provided a checklist of the information you might need to ensure your personal safety and to look after yourself in the aftermath of the end of an abusive relationship. We refer you to the website mentioned above to examine the information and tips about each of these areas.

Self-protection checklist	
In the early stages	
	Learn ways to stay safe online, including using hardware (phones, computers, devices) and online accounts (email, social media, location safety).
	Make a safety plan for yourself, your children and your pets.
	Keep important documents safe or copies of important documents (financial, legal, business).
	Collect any evidence you might need for Family Court applications.
	Prepare your banking details (opening new accounts, freezing and closing joint accounts).
Things to do immediately	
	Explore government assistance and benefits available to you.

	Explore family violence restraining orders.
	Investigate and take advantage of assistance services available in your community.
Rebuilding your life	
	Make sure you are safe at home (safety improvements you can make or Safe at Home programmes you can access).
	Make sure you are safe in public (in public places, at work, when driving).
	Make sure your mail is safe.
	Seek financial support available for people who have experienced family and intimate partner violence.
	Secure safe housing/tenancy.
	Access legal services if needed.
Moving forward	
	Learn to budget.
	Adopt strategies to save some money.
	Explore credit alternatives.
	Learn to manage your debt.
	Understand your tax obligations and tax relief.
	Establish a superannuation/retirement account.
	Explore insurance options.
	Prepare a will.
	Effectively use financial settlements.

Checklist available at elemen.com.au

Manage your anxiety/trauma

Now, we can move on to the psychological aspects of you learning to cope in the aftermath of the breakdown of your abusive relationship. We are going to start by teaching you about your nervous system and how to control it. This is important because most people who have experienced abuse in a relationship have also experienced an impact on their nervous system arousal. So, let's look at how your nervous system works and reacts to stressful events.

What is your nervous system doing?

Your autonomic nervous system (ANS) is the part of your nervous system that drives your functioning. It regulates how your body works and makes adjustments required for you to adapt moment-by-moment.

Your ANS is divided into two parts: the parasympathetic nervous system and the sympathetic nervous system. Your parasympathetic nervous system is the part of your ANS that should drive you most of the time. It ensures everything is ticking along so your body gets what it needs and you can function well.

Your sympathetic nervous system has a specialised function. It is your self-protection system that automatically activates when you are under threat. So, if you were crossing the road and a truck came screaming around the corner, your sympathetic nervous system would activate so that you could quickly and efficiently move out of the way of the truck and reach safety. Adrenaline would release into your system, causing your hands to shake, and your heart rate would increase, but you would reach the safety of the footpath on the other side of the road, and you would be fine. Your brain would then recognise that you are safe, your sympathetic nervous system would turn off, and your parasympathetic nervous system would take over again.

Your sympathetic nervous system is attuned to your brain perceiving signs of threat. It activates when you are at risk of harm and prepares you to deal with that threat. It is an effective self-protection system when you are under threat. Unfortunately, for people who develop an overly sensitive sympathetic nervous system due to repeated exposure to danger and threat, or at times when they are experiencing significant stress in their lives, their sympathetic nervous system will activate at the slightest indication that something is wrong. It will prepare them to deal with the threat. This can occur even when there really is no threat to manage. This is what happens when you are anxious in the absence of an obvious cause of your anxiety or an obvious sign of immediate danger. In effect, your brain cannot distinguish between an external threat (e.g., a truck coming around the corner) and an internal threat (e.g., you thinking worrying or anxiety-provoking thoughts). An overly sensitive nervous system will rely on its self-defence mechanism to protect you from perceived harm.

Your nervous system will also react to events that are crises in your life that do not present the same level of threat as physical abuse, for example. Although the experience of emotional abuse is stressful, this type of abuse itself is not physically threatening to you. Nevertheless, your sympathetic nervous system can be triggered by emotional abuse. As stated, your brain cannot always make a distinction between an external threat to your physical integrity and the threat to your emotional well-being that is internally generated.

Below is a table providing an overview of the activities of the parasympathetic and sympathetic nervous systems.

Table 3: The functions of the parasympathetic and sympathetic nervous systems.

	Parasympathetic	Sympathetic
Eyes	Constricts pupils	Dilates pupils
Salivary glands	Stimulates salivation	Inhibits salivation
Heart	Slows heartbeat	Accelerates heartbeat
Lungs	Constricts bronchi	Dilates bronchi
Stomach	Stimulates digestion	Inhibits digestion
Liver	Stimulates bile release	Simulates glucose release
Kidneys		Stimulates release of adrenaline and noradrenaline*
Intestines	Stimulates peristalsis and secretion	Inhibits peristalsis and secretion
Bladder	Contracts bladder	Relaxes bladder

* Also known as epinephrine and norepinephrine

So, when your sympathetic nervous system is activated, a series of physical changes occur that make sense if they are in response to a threat to your physical integrity.

> Adrenaline is released so that you are alert and in a heightened state, ready to deal with the threat. This causes your heart rate to increase and can cause your hands, or even your whole body, to shake.

> Your hearing and your eyesight become better than normal. Everything sounds louder than it really is, and it is difficult to tolerate lots of light and movement. This is why anxious people tend to avoid places like supermarkets. Too much noise, too much

light, and too much movement can be overwhelming when you feel anxious. Anxious people tend to tolerate these things poorly because of the acuteness of their senses when their sympathetic nervous systems are activated.

In our view, the most amazing thing that happens is that your sympathetic nervous system shuts down the systems it does not need to be using. For example, when under threat, your body needs to produce lots of glucose for energy, so it stimulates glucose production. You use you this glucose quickly when you are in an aroused state. Therefore, other systems that are not needed to protect your from harm are shut down. In particular, your sympathetic nervous system shuts down your gastrointestinal system (e.g., inhibits digestion and inhibits peristalsis and secretion, with peristalsis referring to the contraction of the muscles that push forward the contents of your digestive tract). This is all right if it is shut down for the period of time it takes for you to deal with a truck coming around the corner. If the sympathetic nervous system activation is prolonged, your body copes less well with your gastrointestinal system not functioning. You can lose your appetite, experience nausea, develop diarrhoea or constipation, and you can experience difficulty eating, or you will overeat to try to control the uncomfortable state of your digestive system.

All of these symptoms make sense if you are under threat but become a problem if the activation of your sympathetic nervous system is prolonged. Also, when your sympathetic nervous system is activated for reasons other than obvious threat, you can develop a sense of imminent danger just because your sympathetic nervous system has taken over your functioning. When your sympathetic nervous system is activated, your brain will interpret this as a sign that something is wrong. You will develop an overwhelming feeling that something terrible is about to happen, even in the absence of an identifiable sign of threat.

Later, we will introduce some straightforward ways to better control your sympathetic nervous system so that your anxiety and fear are reduced. You can learn to control the messages you receive because you are worried so that the message is not misinterpreted, and you can avoid the sense that something terrible is going to happen.

Range of arousal

As described earlier, your sympathetic nervous system has likely responded to your current situation as if it was an immediate threat to your physical integrity. When this occurs, you experience a number of physical changes that place your system into a self-protective state. You need strategies that will send a message to your nervous system that you are safe.

Before considering ways to achieve this, we need to look at one other feature of your nervous system. It is worth noting that human beings have a range of nervous system arousal within which we function the best. This range is quite large, from low in the range when we are very relaxed to high in the range when our nervous system is most 'revved up' but still manageable. Pictured below is a diagram of this arousal range. The range within which you function best is known as the *window of tolerance*.

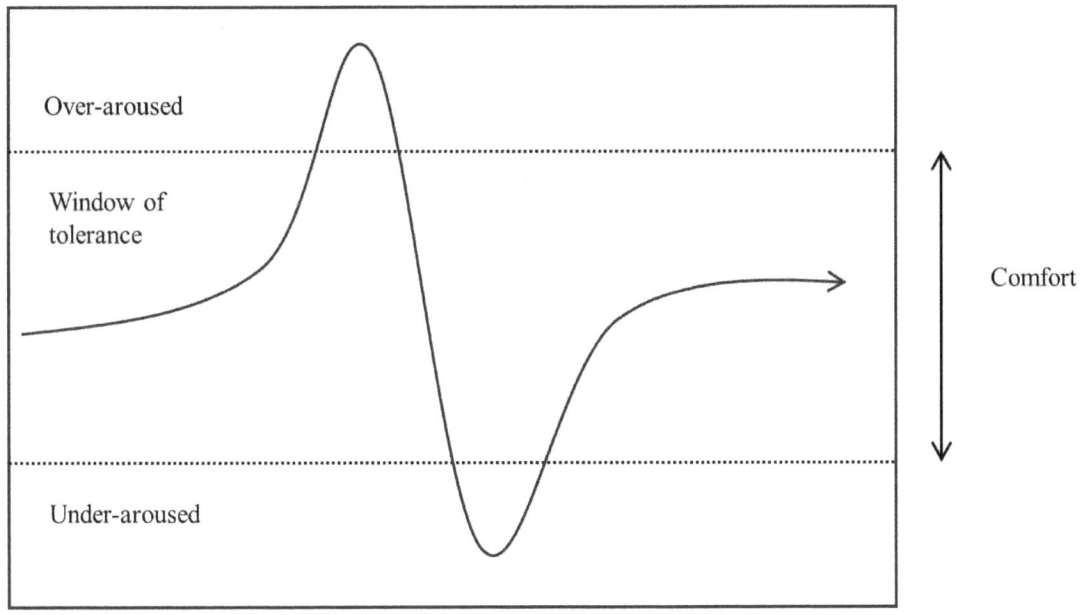

Figure 1: A diagram of the window of tolerance.

Within this window of tolerance, you have the flexibility to respond to the demands being placed on you. In this way, your arousal level will increase when you are faced with a demand and then decrease when that demand is over. As long as your arousal stays within this window, you will respond well to pressures placed on you.

If your arousal level drops below the lowest point of that range, you will enter a state of hypoarousal when you are under-aroused. In this state, you will feel slowed down and lethargic. Your functioning at this point will be inadequate, and your ability to respond to demands will be poor. If your arousal increases beyond the ceiling level, you will enter a state of hyperarousal when you are over-aroused. When this occurs, you can feel too aroused and can feel anxious and panicky. Your functioning will be impacted, and your ability to cope with pressures will deteriorate.

When you have been too stressed for a while or when you are faced with significant challenges but are still managing to cope, your arousal level creeps up from an optimal level of arousal in the middle of the window of tolerance to the upper extremes. You will find that you cannot or do not reduce that high level of arousal, even when you should be able to let go. This is why people cannot sleep well when they are under pressure. They can never relax enough for their arousal to decrease to a comfortable state. So, your 'baseline' arousal level, the starting point from which you respond to life demands, is high up in the range instead of midway.

In this case, your arousal level remains elevated. You barely notice this because it starts to feel normal to be under that much stress with your arousal level that high. But a problem exists. When any other thing occurs to which you have to respond, your arousal level will increase to deal with that additional demand being placed on you. However, when the starting point of your arousal level, or your baseline arousal level, is already so high, you have no room to move. Any increase in arousal will push you through the ceiling and into an uncomfortable and unpleasant hyperaroused state. You will experience anxiety as a result.

Your high starting point gives you no flexibility to respond or react to even minor additional stressors. So, the ways you normally cope with demanding situations fail because you have moved out of the range where you can successfully apply your usual coping strategies.

Anxiety management strategies

Your goal should be to get your nervous system back under control. Dealing with the challenges you have faced in relation to the abuse you experienced has likely pushed your arousal level to the upper limits of your window of tolerance. Extra demands, even minor ones, then cause your arousal level to move beyond the ceiling of the window of tolerance and uncomfortable and unpleasant anxiety symptoms are then experienced.

You need to aim to bring your optimal arousal level down to at least the middle of the window of tolerance, with a baseline or starting point, when you are at your most relaxed, to the lower end of that range. You need to teach your nervous system to have a better starting point and a better optimal arousal level.

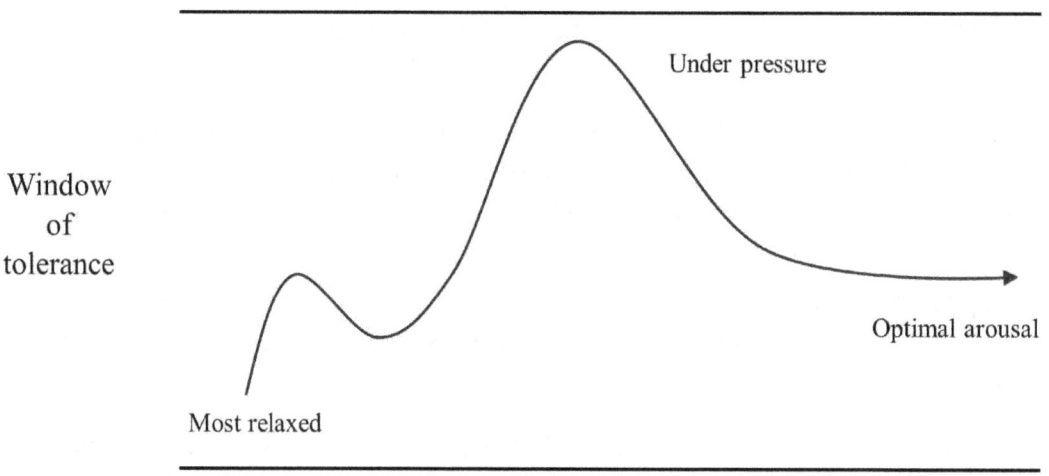

Figure 2: A diagram of your optimal level of arousal.

How do you achieve this? Consider the following. When you are in an elevated or heightened state, at the top of your window of tolerance or beyond it, your heart rate increases and your breathing changes. Your heart rate elevation is caused by a release of adrenaline that occurs when your sympathetic nervous system is triggered. This can be very uncomfortable, and it feels like there is very little you can do about it. However, there are things you can do to bring this under control.

Your breathing changes contribute to the elevation in your heart rate. When people are stressed, their breathing tends to be rapid and shallow. You can liken this pattern of breathing to the waves on top of the water. Form a picture in your mind of the way a child draws waves. When we are stressed, we tend to breathe in sharply, then breathe out quickly and then breathe in again quickly. You tend not to breathe all the way out before you breathe in again. This inhalation-exhalation pattern is what affects your heart rate.

In contrast, when we are relaxed, our breathing tends to be deeper and slower and has a pattern similar to the swell in the ocean. The inhalation-exhalation pattern is a comfortable breath-in followed by a long, slower breath-out. You do not breathe in again until you have breathed all the way out.

From the diagram below, you can see the pattern of anxious, rapid, and shallow breathing at the top and the pattern of slower, deeper breathing characteristic of a more relaxed state below.

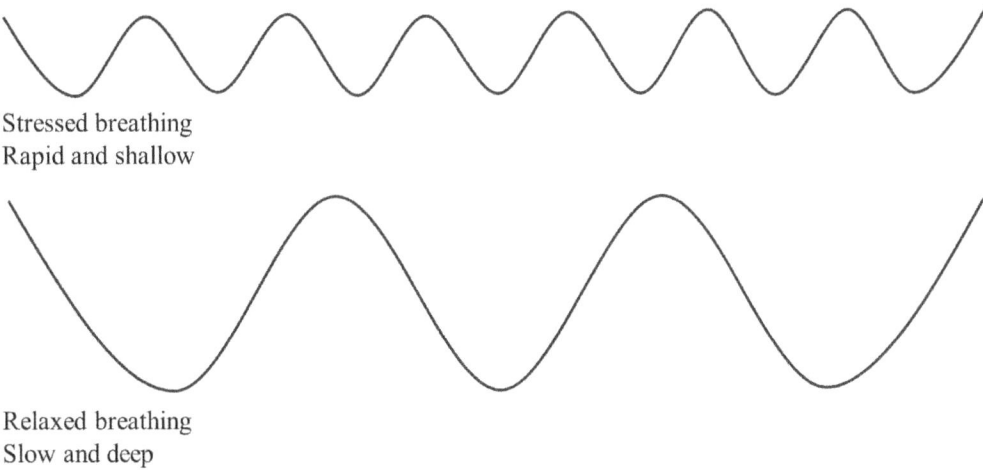

Figure 3: A comparison between stressed and relaxed breathing.

Your breathing pattern affects your heart rate because these two things are linked. Under normal, stress-free conditions, your heart rate increases as you breathe in and then slows as you breathe out. This is normal. When you are stressed, your respiration rate increases and your breathing is shallower. Your heart rate does not have a chance to slow before you breathe in again. Therefore, your heart rate is elevated and stays elevated.

Let's, for a moment, go back to the truck speeding around the corner, threatening to run you over. Your sympathetic nervous system is activated, allowing you to be in the right physical state to move quickly out of harm's way and protect yourself. When you get to the other side of the road, the truck goes past, and you are unharmed, your brain registers these experiences, and your sympathetic nervous system turns off, and your parasympathetic nervous system takes over. This is because reaching the other side of the road and seeing the truck pass you by are safety signals. Your brain interprets these signs as indicators that you will be all right as danger has passed.

Of course, no such safety signals are available when you are sitting in your loungeroom worrying or shopping at the supermarket. They are not that sort of event. Also, there are no safety signals available when your nervous system has learned to be on alert because of abuse in a relationship. Your brain would struggle to identify safety indicators because they do not exist in that form. Even after the abusive relationship is over, your nervous system is slow to get the message you are safe. It has been on red alert for so long that it does not know how to let go. What you can do when this has occurred is to offer your brain a safety signal but of a different type.

You can send a message that everything is all right by deliberately slowing your heart rate from its elevated rate to a more normal rate for you. Although it sounds difficult to achieve, controlling your heart rate is actually a reasonably straightforward undertaking. If you slow your breathing and lengthen your exhalation until you have breathed all the way out before breathing back in, your heart rate will come into line with your breathing rate, and your heart rate will go down.

To use our waves and ocean swell analogy, the aim is to change your breathing pattern from waves on the top of the water to a pattern like the swell in the ocean, where the water is lifted up and then put back down as the swell passes. You are aiming for an easy, comfortable breath in, followed by a long, slow breath out.

The ideal situation is to breathe out for twice as long as it takes you to breathe in. Elongating your exhalation requires that you slow the amount of air you breathe out so that you can breathe out for longer. You should aim to breathe all the way out, emptying your lungs, before you gently and comfortably breathe back in.

This breathing pattern should result in a slowed heart rate and a subsequent reduction in that sense of anxiety or crisis that occurs when your sympathetic nervous system is triggered. This occurs because your brain interprets the reduction in heart rate and the change in breathing pattern as a signal that the crisis is over.

Let's consider a simple exercise to control your breathing by deepening your breaths and slowing them down.

	Slowing and controlling your breathing
1.	Without trying to change your breathing, just notice for a moment the pattern of your inhalations and exhalations.
2.	Now, take a comfortable breath in. It does not have to be too deep, rather just a comfortable breath.
3.	Now, breathe out, slowing the amount of air you exhale and lengthening your breath as a result.
4.	When your lungs feel empty of air, gently and comfortably breathe back in.
5.	As you breathe, practice lengthening your exhalation just a bit. You may also deepen your breath in slightly. If this helps, remember the picture of the ocean swell.
6.	Practice this pattern of breathing for as long as you feel comfortable.

Exercise available at elemen.com.au

You can add another element to this breathing exercise that may help with your ultimate goal of reducing your anxiety and signalling your sympathetic nervous system to turn off so your parasympathetic nervous system can do its job. You can include the element of reducing your muscle tension in this breathing exercise.

People who are stressed tend to have tense muscles. Although this muscle tension can occur anywhere in the body, common sites include the forehead, scalp, neck, jaw, shoulders, and chest. The increased muscle tension contributes to the overall sense of readiness to deal with threat. On the downside, tense muscles can cause headaches, chest and other pain.

If tense muscles present a significant problem for you, a progressive muscle relaxation exercise may help. A general overview of this technique is provided below, along with a more comprehensive version. However, another easy strategy is to link the relaxation of muscles with the breathing exercise.

As you breathe out, just relax your muscles in places where they feel tight and tense. You do not have to achieve marked muscle relaxation to experience a noticeable difference. Drop your shoulders, relax your jaw, smooth your forehead or relax your stomach muscles. Aim for a gentle relaxation of tight muscles as you exhale.

Combining breathing exercise and muscle relaxation can be used even when focusing on controlling your breathing. You can also use the combined technique when your primary focus is on troubling muscle tension. In combination, the techniques can help with either target.

Combined breathing and muscle relaxation technique	
1.	Take a comfortable breath in. It does not have to be too deep, rather just a comfortable breath.
2.	Now, breathe out, slowing the amount of air you exhale and lengthening your breath. As you breathe out, drop your shoulders, relax your jaw, smooth your forehead, and relax your abdominal muscles.
3.	When your lungs feel empty of air, gently and comfortably breathe back in.
4.	As you breathe, practice lengthening your exhalation just a bit. You may also deepen your breath in slightly. Keep in mind the picture of the ocean swell if this helps. Continue to relax your muscles slightly on each exhalation.
5.	Practice this breathing and muscle relaxation pattern for as long as you feel comfortable.

Exercise available at elemen.com.au

As stated, if muscle tension presents you with a significant problem, you may wish to try a method of progressive muscle relaxation. People with muscle tension problems often feel pain from strained muscles, tension headaches, pain in the neck and shoulders, and sore muscles across the chest. To address this problem, we will start with a longer version to help you learn the technique. You can then change to a shorter version, which we describe below.

Progressive muscle relaxation (longer version)	
1.	Choose a quiet, comfortable place. Lay down or sit in a comfortable position with your feet flat on the floor.
2.	Now, clench both your fists… tighter and tighter. Notice the tension in your muscles. Keep them clenched for about 10 seconds. Now relax. Feel your muscles relax. Notice the difference between the tension and relaxation.
3.	Repeat the procedure with your fists. Notice the difference between tension and relaxation.
4.	Now, bend your elbows on both arms and tense your biceps. Hold the tension. Now relax. Notice the difference between tension and relaxation.

5.	Repeat the procedure with your elbows bent and your biceps tensed. Hold the tension, then relax. Pay attention to the change from tension to relaxation.
6.	Now, frown as hard as you can. Notice the tension in your forehead. Hold the tension. Now relax. Notice the difference you feel after you have released the tension.
7.	Now, frown again as hard as you can. Hold the tension, then release it. Notice the contrast between tension and relaxation.
8.	Now, close your eyes and squint them tightly. Hold the tension, then relax. Allow your eyes to achieve a comfortable, relaxed state. Notice the change. Repeat by closing your eyes and squinting, then relaxing and letting go of the tension.
9.	Now, clench your jaw. Bite down. Notice the tension throughout your jaw. Now, relax your jaw, allowing your teeth to fall apart slightly. Notice the feeling of relaxation. Repeat this exercise with your jaw.
10.	Now, press your tongue hard against the roof of your mouth. Hold it there. Feel the tension at the back of your mouth. Now relax. Notice the difference between the tension and relaxation. Repeat the exercise with your tongue.
11.	Now, purse your lips, pushing them out into an 'O' shape. Hold them there. Now, release the tension and relax. Notice how your mouth feels now that it is relaxed. Repeat the exercise with your lips.
12.	Now, press your head back as far as it will comfortably go. Hold onto the tension. Roll your head from the right to the left, allowing the focus of the tension to change. Now relax. Feel the difference between the tension in your neck and the relaxation. Repeat the exercise by pressing your head back.
13.	Now, bring your head forward with your chin on your chest. Feel the tension in your throat and the back of your neck. Hold the tension, then relax and allow your head to return to a comfortable position. Repeat the exercise by bringing your head forward.
14.	Now, shrug your shoulders, bringing your shoulders up and allowing your head to hunch down between them. Hold the tension. Now relax and notice the difference between tension and relaxation.
15.	Now, breathe in deeply and hold your breath. Hold it. Now, allow yourself to exhale gently, letting go of tension as you breathe out. Feel your body relax. Repeat the exercise, breathing in and gently letting go.

16.	Now, tense your stomach muscles. Hold onto the tension. Now relax. Let your stomach muscles relax and appreciate that feeling. Repeat the exercise with your stomach muscles.
17.	Now, arch your back without straining. Hold onto the tension. Now, let it go. Notice the change in your muscles. Repeat the exercise by arching your back.
18.	Now, tighten your buttocks and thighs. Press down on your heels to flex your thigh muscles. Hold onto the tension. Now relax and notice the difference. Repeat the exercise.
19.	Now, curl your toes downward to cause your calves to tense. Hold onto the tension. Now relax. Repeat the exercise.
20.	Now, draw your toes upward, causing your shins to feel tense. Pay attention to the tension. Now relax. Repeat the exercise.
21.	Now, scan your body. Notice if there are any tense spots. Repeat the exercise in that area.
22.	Enjoy the more relaxed feeling throughout your entire body. When you are ready, slowly return to your normal activities, holding on to that feeling of relaxation.

Exercise available at elemen.com.au

Once you have learned the technique, you can use a shorter version. You may prefer to just focus on the areas of your body that are particularly tense. It is certainly the case that some people tend to carry their muscle tension in one or two areas. Here is a shorter version that will allow you to tailor the procedure to suit your own needs.

	Relaxing using progressive muscle relaxation (short version)
1.	Choose a quiet, comfortable place. Lay down or sit in a comfortable position with your feet flat on the floor.
2.	Begin to work your way through groups of muscles by tensing and relaxing them. For example, if you start with your forehead, tighten the muscles by frowning. Hold for a few moments (10-15 seconds), then release, allowing the muscle in your forehead to relax. Enjoy that experience for about 60 seconds. Notice the difference between the tension and the relaxation.
3.	Then, move on to the next group of muscles. You can work through groups of muscles from the top of your head to the tips of your toes, or you can select areas of your body that present a particular problem of tension for you.
4.	Repeat the process until you have worked your way through the groups of muscles you have selected.
5.	Repeat that process, first tensing the muscles, holding that tension for five to ten seconds, and then relaxing those muscles.

Exercise available at elemen.com.au

So, controlling your breathing and, thus, lowering your heart rate will help you feel less anxious, as will reducing your muscle tension. However, there are other approaches you can take to anxiety management.

Quietening your mind

One of the problems with being anxious and 'revved up' is that your mind fills up with anxiety-provoking thoughts. When you have experienced abuse and, indeed, when you continue to fear the abuser, you cannot seem to stop thinking in an endless stream of anxiety-provoking thoughts. This makes it very difficult to get your nervous system back under control. The thoughts racing through your mind do not allow you to relax. So, included here are some exercises that should help you settle your mind.

The first exercises aim to teach you to self-soothe. If you can learn to settle yourself, the racing thoughts in your mind may follow. The quieter your nervous system, the less active your mind is with anxiety-provoking thoughts.

You are aiming to find ways to soothe yourself. Most of us can understand how we soothe an upset child. We might hold and rock a distressed child and say soothing things. What you are looking for are versions of self-soothing strategies that will help you, as an adult, alleviate your distressed state.

Developing self-soothing strategies aims to create moments of less distress for yourself. The strategies aim to reduce your heightened state to a more manageable level. They allow your nervous system arousal level to be brought back under your control. So, strategies that enable you to focus on the here and now are the ones that will allow you to choose to be in a quieter state with a greater sense of peace of mind.

Consider the proposed self-soothing strategies listed below and select ones that you think might assist you. These may be things you have tried before or ones you feel might work for you. Some of these strategies require you to make an effort to seek out the means of engaging with them. However, others are using things that are readily available or easily obtained.

	Self-soothing strategies
	Take a shower or a warm bath. Focus your attention on the sensations created by the water. Enjoy the feeling of the water on your skin and the warmth of the water. Turn your mind off to other thoughts and focus on the water and its warmth.
	Play with your pet, or just stroke your dog's or cat's coat. Interacting with your pet has been demonstrated to be soothing for many pet owners.
	Change into your most comfortable clothes. Enjoy the feel of the fabric and the degree of comfort you feel from wearing these items of clothing.
	Go for a swim. Enjoy the sensation of being in the water. Allow those sensations to quiet your mind. Even if you are not a good swimmer, bobbing around in the water can produce the same sensations.
	Treat yourself to a massage if that appeals to you. Allow your muscles to relax and your mind to quiet.
	Listen to soothing music. Allow your attention to be directed to the music rather than having it in the background.
	Listen to an audiobook, even if your distress makes it difficult to concentrate. Try to pay attention to each word that is spoken. If you lose track of the story, you can always return to the previous track and pick up the story again.
	Turn on the television or talkback radio and listen to what is being broadcast. The goal is to focus your attention on the conversations as they play out rather than selecting a programme you are excited to watch or listen to. Focusing on other people talking can be soothing.

| | Listen to the sounds of water running. Again, the aim is to listen to the sounds of the water, stopping your mind from going to other intrusive thoughts. You can find the sound of running water in various places. You can visit a naturally occurring water course or waterfall. You could listen to running water from an outdoor garden fountain. However, you can also get an indoor personal fountain that can be used anytime. Alternatively, you can listen to recorded sounds of water running. |
| | Find something soothing to look at. This might be by the water or an outdoor space like a park. It could be photographs or paintings that you find soothing or relaxing. The goal is to find something to look at that is engaging and that you find relaxing and soothing. |

Exercise available at elemen.com.au

Building on this notion of self-soothing, it is a good idea to be more present in your focus. If you consider it, you will find that the thoughts racing through your mind when you are anxious typically are unrelated to what is happening in the here and now. Our thoughts tend to engage in time-travelling, that is, they are focused either on what has already happened or what is to come. They rarely focus on what is happening in the present moment when you are trying to relax.

Usually, at these times, nothing is happening that is worth worrying about. If you could deliberately spend more time focused on the here and now and less time on the past or future, you would have a better chance of relaxing and quieting your overly stimulated nervous system.

The suggestion of focusing on the here and now is based on the notion of mindfulness. Mindfulness refers to your ability to be aware of your emotions, physical state, actions, and thoughts in a state of mind that is absent from judgment or criticism of your experience. Research has demonstrated that mindfulness helps you control symptoms of anxiety, control the distress caused by particular situations, increase your capacity to relax, and learn how to cope better with challenging situations.

Based on the notion of mindfulness, we have included some exercises you can use to quiet your mind by focusing on the here and now. To do this well, you may need to practice the skill. When you first learn these techniques, it is easy to become distracted and return to your racing thoughts. Do not worry if this happens. Just return to your exercise and continue.

	Mindful listening
1.	Sit in a comfortable place, preferably by yourself. If you wish, close your eyes.
2.	Start to focus your attention on the sounds around you. Identify each sound.
3.	Notice the changes in the sounds from moment to moment.
4.	Notice the times between sounds when it is quiet.
5.	Focus your attention both on what is happening inside and outside.
6.	Pay attention to the sounds and nothing else. Do not make judgments about the sounds. Just acknowledge the sound, then listen to the next one.
7.	If thoughts about other things come into your mind, put them aside and then return to listening to the sounds around you.
8.	Do this for a few minutes or until you are ready to stop.

Exercise available at elemen.com.au

Let's try another mindfulness exercise.

	Mindful use of your senses
Sight	Look around you. Allow your attention to be drawn to five things in your immediate environment that you might not normally pay any attention to. For example, this might be the way the fruit is sitting in the fruit bowl, the way your curtain is hanging, or the way your books are placed on your bookcase. Allow your attention to rest on each of these things. Keep your focus directed at the item, setting aside any other thoughts that come into your mind.
Touch	Bring your attention to four things you can feel at this moment in time. For example, it may be the feel of the sun on your skin, the feel of the fabric of your clothes against your skin, the feel of the chair underneath you, or the feel of the table surface where your hand is resting. Allow your attention to rest on each of these feelings. Keep your focus directed at each sense of touch, setting aside any other thoughts that come into your mind.

Hearing	Listen to the sounds in your surroundings. Notice three things you can hear. For example, you might hear the sounds of cars travelling along the road, the noise of the refrigerator, or the sound of the wind in the trees. Focus your attention on each of these sounds. If other thoughts come into your mind, let those thoughts go and return to focusing on the sounds you can hear.
Smell	Pay attention and search for two things you can smell. For example, you might be able to smell whatever you are cooking, the scent of plants in your garden, or the sea air if you live near the water. Keep your attention focused on each of these smells. If other distracting thoughts come into your mind, let these thoughts go and return to focusing on the things you can smell.
Taste	When you are eating, focus your attention on the tastes you are experiencing. For example, take a sip of your coffee and notice the taste. Bite into your sandwich and notice the flavours. Really pay attention to the flavours of the things you are tasting. If you become distracted, let go of these interfering thoughts and return to focusing on the things you are tasting.

Exercise available at elemen.com.au

And here is one last mindfulness exercise.

Mindful walking	
1.	As you are ready for your walk, stand still for a moment. Sense the weight on your feet as you stand there. Feel how your muscles are supporting you and maintaining your stability and balance. Notice that your arms are in a comfortable position of your choice (e.g., by your side or hands clasped at the front or back). Allow yourself to stand there, relaxed but alert.
2.	Begin to walk. Choose a comfortable pace, not too fast and not too slow. Pay attention to how your feet and legs feel (e.g., their heaviness or lightness, energy, or even any pain). The way your legs and feet feel will form the focus of your attention. If you become distracted, return to focusing on your legs and feet.
3.	Pay attention to how you lift your feet and place them back down on the surface you are walking on. Notice how you lift your foot, swing your leg and place your foot down again ahead of where you were a moment before. Walk in a natural and relaxed manner. Move your arms in a way that feels normal for you.

4.	It is likely that your mind will wander as you walk along. Your attention will be drawn to what is around you or thoughts that come into your mind. Acknowledge that you have been distracted and return to focusing on the process of walking… the lifting of your foot, the swing of your leg and the placement of your foot in front of you. Just gently return your attention to the sensations of walking.
5.	You might focus on a point ahead of you. Focus on the steps you take as you move towards that point, one step at a time, and experience fully the sensations of walking.
6.	Keep walking mindfully until you reach your destination or the point where you decide to turn around and mindfully walk back to where you started.

Exercise available at elemen.com.au

These types of strategies can help deal with another manifestation of too much stress and too much anxiety, that is, sleep disturbance. Let's consider this next.

Dealing with sleep disturbance

One of the consequences of your nervous system being revved up and having too many stressful thoughts is that your sleep can become disturbed. You can become fatigued as a consequence, and it becomes more difficult for you to cope with the demands of your day.

There are three types of insomnia. You might experience any one or all three of these types of sleep problems.

> *Trouble going to sleep.* This is where you are unable to go to sleep despite being tired.
>
> *Trouble staying asleep.* This is where you repeatedly wake throughout the night, but after a period of time, you are able to go back to sleep.
>
> *Waking early and being unable to go back to sleep.* This is when you wake early in the morning and, despite needing more sleep, cannot return to sleep.

Each of these types of sleep problems is understandable if you consider your sleep stages.

Table 4: A description of the stages of sleep.

Stages of sleep	
Stage 1	This is a transitional stage from wakefulness to sleep. It is associated with very light sleep. During this stage, muscle activity slows down.
Stage 2	During this stage, your sleep starts to deepen. Your breathing pattern changes and slows, and so does your heart rate. Your body temperature drops slightly.
Stage 3	It is at this stage that deep sleep begins to be experienced. To signal the onset of deep sleep, your brain starts to generate slow delta waves.
Stage 4	This is when you are most deeply asleep. During this stage, your muscle activity is limited.
REM sleep	This refers to Rapid Eye Movement Sleep. It occurs when you are at the closest point to wakefulness. It is associated with vivid dreaming. During this stage, your heart rate increases.

Over the course of the night, you will cycle through these stages. For the first half or so of the night, you will cycle down into the deep sleep associated with stages 3 and 4. However, as the night progresses, the cycling pattern is lighter and does not involve deep sleep. This pattern is demonstrated in the diagram below. Periods of REM sleep occur at the point in the cycle when you are closest to waking.

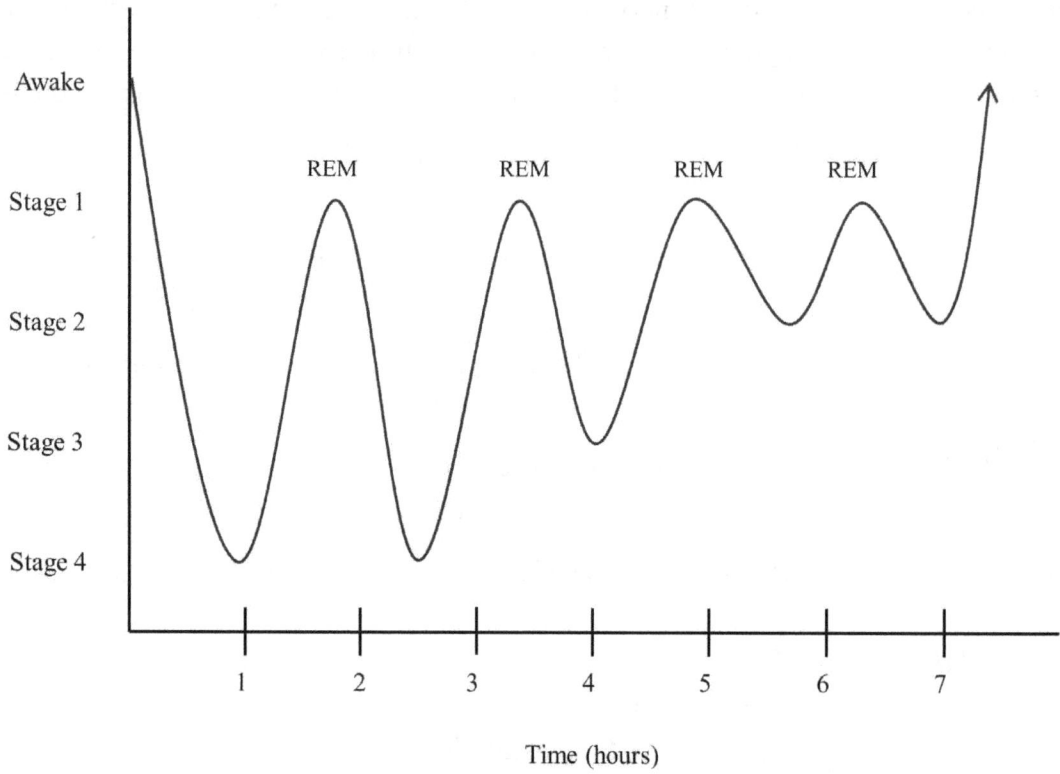

Figure 4: The cycles of sleep over the course of a sleep period.

When you have trouble falling asleep at the beginning of the night, you are struggling to enter into Stage 1 of sleep. This transitional stage is designed to pull you down into deeper sleep. Stage 1 allows you to do what your brain is inviting you to do, that is, go to sleep. Unfortunately, if you are stressed, your nervous system is generally too aroused to allow this to occur. Your nervous system fights against this natural urge to sleep. Your stressful thoughts are indicating to your brain that it is a good idea to stay awake in case something happens to which you need to respond.

When you have trouble staying asleep, you tend to wake up when your sleep cycle reaches the points closest to wakefulness. In general, your nervous system is too aroused to allow you to stay asleep. Then, as soon as you wake, your mind turns to stressful thoughts that keep you awake until you can get back to sleep. This can happen many times throughout the night.

When you are troubled by waking early and being unable to return to sleep, this usually occurs in the second part of the night when you have moved past the deep sleep cycles. Your sleep is lighter, and when your nervous system is too aroused and you come close to wakefulness, you become completely awake, your stressful thoughts begin, and you cannot get back to sleep.

What can I do about my sleep problems?

Racing thoughts can influence each of these types of sleep disturbance. These thoughts are usually stressful and increase nervous system arousal, making it difficult to get any rest.

Here is a series of simple steps that can help you have a better night's sleep.

	Simple sleep strategy
1.	In the evening, avoid caffeine and sugary drinks and food.
2.	In the lead-up to bedtime, start to wind down. Turn off stimulating television or stop engaging in other activities around the house that make you feel more alert.
3.	Have a small snack rich in carbohydrates.
4.	Get into a comfortable bed and a comfortable position. Slow your breathing. Relax your muscle tension.
5.	Give your mind something to think about that is not emotionally arousing. This could be writing a simple story in your head, listing in your mind all the countries you can think of, starting with A, then B, etc. Alternatively, count backwards by 7s from a randomly selected number.
6.	If your thoughts drift to more stressful thoughts, acknowledge what is happening, and then return to the activity you chose to keep your mind focused.
7.	Allow yourself to drift off to sleep.

Exercise available at elemen.com.au

The goal is to create the right internal environment to facilitate a good night's sleep. Avoid caffeine and sugary food or drinks because they can have a stimulating effect on your nervous system. In general, you should aim to 'turn off' by reducing the number of external stimulating activities. You do these things in preparation for sleep.

Carbohydrates can also increase your readiness for sleep. This is because carbohydrates contribute to an increase in your brain of a protein called tryptophan. This is a building block for a neurotransmitter called serotonin and a hormone called melatonin. Serotonin has a role in controlling sleep, appetite and mood. Melatonin release is triggered by darkness, and this hormone helps promote a regular sleep-wake cycle. This process, encouraged by eating a carbohydrate-rich snack before bedtime, helps you sleep.

When your mind is already overrun by thoughts that are keeping you awake, it seems counterintuitive to give your brain something else to think about. However, it is not the thoughts themselves that will keep you awake. It is the nature of the thoughts that will affect your sleep. In this way, you want to distract yourself from thinking stress-related thoughts, replacing them with thoughts that will not cause you to react emotionally. You should aim to keep your brain busy with mundane thoughts so that your mind is distracted from the stress-inducing thoughts. We refer to this activity as 'busy work' for your brain. It is the modern-day equivalent of counting sheep.

Mundane thoughts will allow you to drift off to sleep, whereas stress-related thoughts will keep you alert and awake. Your brain is always active, so it is not possible to stop thinking. When you think of things that cause your nervous system to respond by increasing your arousal, you will have trouble sleeping. If you think calming or even boring thoughts, your brain will trigger the processes that lead you to fall asleep.

If you awaken during the night, the same strategy of giving your mind something other than stressful things to think about can be applied. Simply get settled and focus on your selected mundane thoughts, allowing yourself to drift off to sleep.

Learning to regulate your emotional state is necessary as an overall strategy for allowing yourself to feel more settled. We will consider how to do this next.

Regulating your emotions

Experiencing a stressful time, such as would occur when you leave an abusive relationship, can result in a period of strong, volatile and variable emotions. This is a difficult and uncomfortable time. Although it is quite normal to have this type of reaction, and you cannot really avoid it altogether, the aim should be to reduce the severity of your distress and shorten the duration of this challenging period if you can do so.

This does not mean that you should fight against the emotions you feel. You cannot start a war with your emotional state and expect to be the victor. You cannot ignore your emotions and expect them just to disappear. The aim should be to recognise and validate your emotional reactions but do what you can to avoid escalating emotional distress.

One way to do this is to focus your attention and coping efforts on your presenting emotional state. For example, if you feel anxious, then give this emotion your attention and work on ways to cope with it. The anxiety you are feeling is your primary emotion at that time. It is the emotion you feel directly because of what has happened to you.

It sounds straightforward. However, human beings are complex creatures who have the capacity to make themselves feel even more miserable. We experience different secondary emotions as a result of our reaction to the primary emotion. Let's consider how this might work with your anxious feelings in the aftermath of the end of the abusive relationship.

What happened?	*I left an abusive relationship.*
How do you feel?	*I feel anxious* (primary emotion).
How do you react to the anxiety?	*I don't like feeling anxious, and I want it to go away.*
What do you say to yourself?	*"I hate feeling anxious."* *"I should be able to control this feeling."*
What do you feel then?	*I feel self-critical* (secondary emotion).
How do you react to this feeling?	*I don't like the feeling, and I want it to go away.*
What do you say to yourself?	*"Here I am blaming myself."* *"I am just making things worse for myself."*

What do you feel then?	*I feel annoyed* (secondary emotion).
How do you react to this feeling?	*I feel uncomfortable and stressed.*
What do you say to yourself?	*"I am feeling so bad I will never get over this."*
What do you feel then?	*I feel despairing* (secondary emotion).

So now, instead of only feeling anxious, you feel anxious, self-critical, annoyed and despairing. Your primary emotion of anxiety was directly related to the problem situation that triggered the emotional reaction. The secondary emotions of self-criticism, annoyance and despair all developed as a result of your reaction to the primary emotion, that is, your anxiety.

Your emotional reactions can be difficult to manage because what started as a straightforward emotional response to a stressful event turns into a confusing array of emotions. Sometimes, these emotions can compete with each other and pull you in different directions. For example, you can feel both sad and angry, or angry and excited. Trying to deal with one of these emotions can be undermined by your efforts to deal with the other emotion.

When dealing with difficult life events, simplifying things is necessary. You can learn to focus on your primary emotions as they arise and adopt strategies to deal with them. Let's start by looking at a way to identify your emotions so you know what to give your attention to.

Recognising and dealing with your emotions

Let's start by taking the process of experiencing an emotional reaction a step at a time.

What happened?

Here, consider the situation that developed, resulting in you feeling these strong emotions. Identify specific details of what happened rather than talking in generalised terms (e.g., "I never cope", "I always make mistakes").

Why did this situation occur?

Consider the possible causes of the problem situation. This is an important step. It gives you the opportunity to interpret the meaning of the problem situation in an effort to help you understand why you are feeling the strong emotions you are experiencing.

How were you feeling as a result of this situation?

Try to identify your primary emotional response to the situation and then consider the secondary emotions you experience as well.

What is it that you wanted to do *as a result of how you were feeling?*

Here, we refer to the urges or impulses you have to act in response to your emotional state. When feeling strong emotions, people tend to experience urges to do more extreme actions.

It does not follow that you will always do these things; however, thoughts about doing them can be present. It is worth noting that people tend to think about doing extreme things much more often than they ever do them. What this means is that you control the impulse to act in an over-the-top way. If you can control these impulses, you can control others in a way that will allow you to have a more settled and reasonable response to provoking situations.

What did you actually do *and* say?

Here, you are considering what you actually did rather than what you had an urge to do.

After experiencing those emotions and actions, how did they affect you?

Here, we are referring to the consequences of experiencing those strong emotional states and your reactions to those states by choosing to act in a particular way.

To try and make sense of what you are feeling and why you are feeling it, we suggest you use the worksheet below. It is designed to help you understand how you are reacting to the problems you are facing, which may direct you to how you can cope with the situation. First, let's look at how you can use this worksheet.

Understanding your emotions worksheet
Time and date: *Thursday 10th*
What happened? *I was home alone and I started to feel really anxious. I paced around and I couldn't settle.*
Why did this situation occur? *I had shut myself off from everyone for days. By Thursday, I hadn't spoken to anyone and I only had my own thoughts for company.*

How were you feeling as a result of that situation?
I realised I was really alone and that was unsettling. In reaction to that I felt anxious and I couldn't settle down.
What is it that you wanted to do as a result of how you were feeling?
I wanted the anxiety to stop so I thought about calling my ex-partner and asking if he would take me back. That seemed to be a better option than the anxiety I was feeling about being alone.
What did you actually do and say?
I turned on the television and watched that for a while then I went to bed.
After experiencing those emotions and actions, how did they affect you?
I felt empty and alone. The bad anxiety passed but I still felt empty.

Here is the worksheet you can use.

Understanding your emotions worksheet
Time and date:
What happened?
Why did this situation occur?
How were you feeling as a result of this situation?

What is it that you wanted to do as a result of how you were feeling?
What did you actually do and say?
After experiencing those emotions and actions, how did they affect you?

Worksheet available at elemen.com.au

The link between your emotions and your behaviour

It is worthwhile to understand the link between your emotional state and the things you choose to do in response to that emotion. This is important. It is difficult to control your behaviour choices if you do not appreciate the link between how you feel and what you do.

Let's consider how you might behave in relation to your emotional responses. Consider this example.

I felt	What I did
Anxious	*I shut myself off from everyone. I paced around at home day and night.*

Understanding this link between your emotional state and your behaviour can help you learn to make different choices in how you act when you are upset. We will explore this further when we consider building your coping strategies, but let's consider here how you might opt to do different things. Consider the same example but now let's look at how this person might have chosen to do things differently.

I felt	What I did	What I could have done instead
Anxious	*I shut myself off from everyone. I paced around at home day and night.*	*I could have reached out to my family for support. I could have contacted a counselling service.*

Let's take this one step further and consider the likely outcomes of the initial behaviour choice and the alternative one.

I felt…	*Anxious*
I did…	*I shut myself off from everyone. I paced around at home day and night.*
What happened?	*I just felt worse and worse.*
A better choice…	*I could have reached out to my family for support. I could have contacted a counselling service.*
Likely outcome…	*I would have felt better much sooner. I know my family would support me and would offer to comfort me. They would likely come around and be with me so I wouldn't feel so anxious and alone. If I contacted a counselling service, I would have received some good advice about how to manage my anxiety.*

Initially, you can work on thinking up alternative and healthier behaviours after the event. This will allow you to learn how to make better choices by considering the different outcomes of various behaviours. It will then become easier to apply this strategy when you feel the emotional reaction so that you can choose the better behaviour at the time and avoid doing things that might feel all right at the time but do not help you in the longer term. Below is a worksheet you can use.

The emotion-behaviour link worksheet	
I feel/felt…	
I did/I felt the urge to do…	
What happened/ what would have happened?	
A better choice…	
Likely outcome…	

Worksheet available at elemen.com.au

Here you have learned to identify your emotional reactions and to respond to them differently, focusing on your primary emotions and responding to your urges to act in a different way. Now we need to focus on building your coping skills so that you can choose to do particular things that will help you overcome difficult times.

Learn to cope

The fact that you will have a strong and seemingly overwhelming emotional response to the end of the abusive relationship you experienced and the fact that you had experienced those abusive episodes requires that you look for ways to cope. That is what we do when we are faced with problem situations in our lives… we try to use the skills we have to cope with our problems.

We all have our own coping resources and individual coping skills. Coping resources are the things we have available to us to help us cope, such as, family and friendships. Coping skills are the strategies we are good at that we use to deal with the problems we face. We have our own particular coping resources and specific coping skills because there is not one particular way of coping.

In a general sense, the way you will cope with this experience will likely be a reflection of the way you have dealt with and solved other problems throughout your life. That is, the way you cope will reflect your general style of coping.

Your goal should be to understand how you cope and to make good use of the coping resources you have or can create, and the particular coping skills you have developed or can develop. This is true even if you take into account the fact that what you are experiencing at the moment may be a more challenging problem than other problems you have dealt with in your life. For those of you who feel they do not cope well with life problems, it may be the case you have been trying to develop coping skills based on a pattern of coping skills that do not suit you.

To understand the way you cope and to use this knowledge to choose the best strategies to cope with the end of the abusive relationship and to promote your recovery from the experiences you have had, consideration needs to be given to the fundamental differences people can have in the way they approach problem situations. Let's consider the different approaches to coping so that you can work out your own preferred coping style.

Problem-focused coping vs. emotion-focused coping

To start, a distinction can be made between problem-focused coping strategies and emotion-focused strategies.

Who are problem-focused copers?

Problem-focused copers deal with their problems by considering the problem situation. They tend to want to *do* something when they are confronted with a problem. They are most comfortable when there are specific things related to the problem that can be the focus of their attention. These people just want to *do* something to fix the problem.

Who are emotion-focused copers?

Emotion-focused copers are the people who deal with their problems by expressing their emotional reactions to the situation. They will talk about the problem and cry when they feel the need. They see the value of looking to others to share their feelings about their problem. In the context of the situation they are facing, the emotion-focused coper will say "I need to talk about how I am feeling".

Are people either emotion-focused or problem-focused copers?

Some people are strongly problem-focused copers and some people are strongly emotion-focused copers. All others fall somewhere on the continuum between the two extreme positions. You may be more problem-focused than emotion-focused in your coping but still make use of some emotion-focused strategies… or the reverse.

You will be able to do a little exercise to find your coping preferences or to confirm them if you already have a good idea of where on the continuum you fall. But, first, we have to consider one other element.

Problem-approach vs. problem-avoidance coping

People assume that if we talk about coping strategies, they have to be good ones that will help us deal with the problems we face. This is not the case. People's coping style can be divided on the basis of whether they tend to front up to their problems or whether they prefer to avoid them. This is the case for both problem-focused copers and emotion-focused copers.

Let's start by looking at problem-focused coping. How would problem approach and problem avoidance strategies differ? Consider the examples in the table below.

Table 5: Examples of problem-focused approach and avoidance strategies.

Problem-focused approach strategies	Problem-focused avoidance strategies
Problem solving Problem solving coping strategies involve: Examining the problem Generating potential solutions Evaluating the likelihood of a successful outcome Moving forward and applying the strategy	*Problem avoidance* Problem avoidance coping strategies involve: Deliberately avoiding thinking about the problem Deliberately avoiding reminders of the problem
Cognitive restructuring Cognitive restructuring coping strategies involve: Reframing your thoughts to think more reasonably about the problem Correcting errors in thinking that are barriers to coping with the problem	*Wishful thinking* Wishful thinking as a coping strategy involves: Wishing the problem would go away Indulging in thoughts that things will just return to 'normal' Spending time thinking about how things will work out in your favour and as you wish

With regard to you having to deal with the aftermath of an abusive relationship, the effective, problem-focused approach coping strategies may help in the following ways. They may help you think clearly about what needs to be done to resolve the situation you are facing. They can keep you focused on what you need to do without being overwhelmed by strong emotions. They can help you feel more in control.

Now let's consider emotion-focused coping. The table below details examples of approach and avoidance emotion-focused coping strategies.

Table 6: Examples of emotion-focused approach and avoidance strategies.

Emotion-focused approach strategies	Emotion-focused avoidance strategies
Emotional expression Emotional expression as a coping strategy involves: Being open and talking about how you are feeling Allowing yourself to experience your emotional reactions in relation to the problem Using emotional expression as a form of catharsis, letting off steam to allow yourself to feel better for a while	*Self-criticism* Self-criticism as a coping strategy involves: Blaming yourself for the problem Criticising yourself for failing to control your emotional reaction to the problem Viewing yourself as more generally deficient than is warranted
Social support Using social support as a coping strategy involves: Turning to family and friends for support Talking with your support network about how you are feeling Taking comfort from your support people Allowing your support network to offer instrumental/practical help	*Social withdrawal* Social withdrawal as a copy strategy involves: Cutting yourself off from family and friends Failing to seek professional support when it is needed Refusing assistance offered by the people who wish to help you or would be willing to do so

When we consider you having to deal with the aftermath of an abusive relationship, the effective emotion-focused approach coping strategies may be of assistance to you in the following ways. They can help you feel some relief when you feel overwhelmed by emotion. They can help you take advantage of your support network of family and friends. They can help you deal with the emotional roller coaster ride of emotions you experience with this stressful life event.

Identifying your preferred coping style

The goal here is to identify the type of coping that works best for you. If you are an emotion-focused coper, you may see the value of a problem-focused coping approach. Still, it is unlikely that you could comfortably be able to adopt problem-focused coping strategies and expect them to work for you. Your efforts would be better directed at taking advantage of your preferred coping style and using problem-approach strategies.

Here is an exercise to determine what type of coping style best characterises your preferred type. If you typically use the listed coping strategy, tick the boxes.

	How do I normally cope?
Problem-solving	
	I work on finding ways to solve the problems I face.
	I work out what I should do and then follow the plan.
	I like to work out a plan and then move forward.
	I believe there is a solution to every problem.
Problem avoidance	
	I try to act like nothing is wrong.
	When faced with a problem, I choose not to do anything, even when I know I should.
	I try not to spend any time thinking about the problem.
	When the problem comes to mind, I push it out of my head.
Cognitive restructuring	
	I think about my problems in a way that allows me to realise I can manage them.
	I think about the problem to change the way I react to it.
	I try to look on the bright side of any situation.
	I try to put things into perspective.
Wishful thinking	
	When faced with a problem, I just wish it would go away.

	I just hope a miracle will happen to make everything all right.
	I hope the problem will fix itself.
	I wish that someone would come and fix the problem for me.
Emotion expression	
	When faced with a problem, I allow myself to express my feelings about it.
	I do not try to bottle up my feelings; I let them go so that I can feel better.
	I do not hide my feelings about the problem from other people.
	When faced with a problem, I need time to experience my feelings.
Self-criticism	
	I blame myself for the problem I am facing.
	I ask myself what I have done to make the problem happen.
	I tend to hold myself responsible for the problems I face.
	When a problem occurs, I feel I should have done things differently.
Social support	
	I turn to the people I know will listen when I talk about how I feel.
	I feel better when I can talk to others about my problems.
	When faced with a problem, I seek advice from people I trust.
	I allow other people to offer help and support when I am dealing with a problem.

	Social withdrawal
	When faced with a problem, I like to avoid other people and spend time by myself.
	When I am struggling with a problem, I do not want to be around other people.
	I do not share my thoughts and feelings with others.
	I do not accept the help others offer.

Checklist available at elemen.com.au

What type of coper are you? Add up the ticks you have placed in each of the categories and enter the number in the following table.

Ways of coping score sheet	
Problem-focused strategies	*Emotion-focused strategies*
_____ Problem-solving _____ Cognitive restructuring _____ Problem avoidance _____ Wishful thinking _____ **Total**	_____ Emotion expression _____ Social support _____ Self-criticism _____ Social withdrawal _____ **Total**
Problem-approach strategies	*Problem-avoidance strategies*
_____ Problem-solving _____ Cognitive restructuring _____ Emotion expression _____ Social support _____ **Total**	_____ Problem-avoidance _____ Wishful thinking _____ Self-criticism _____ Social withdrawal _____ **Total**

Score sheet available at elemen.com.au

When comparing your problem-focused and emotion-focused strategies, see where you have scored the highest. This may show a strong preference for one type of coping strategy or the other. If so, you can build on your preferred coping type when considering what coping strategies will help you with your current situation. If you have similar totals for problem-focused and emotion-focused strategies, you would best include each type in your coping plan.

When considering whether you use problem-approach strategies or problem-avoidance strategies, you are considering whether adjustments must be made in how you cope. If you predominantly use problem-avoidance strategies, you can learn to abandon those in favour of problem-approach strategies while staying within the same style of coping strategy, that is, problem-focused or emotion-focused.

We will now consider how to fully take advantage of your coping strategies, building on problem-approach strategies and letting go of problem-avoidance strategies.

Building your coping repertoire

As you better understand how you cope, you can start to build a plan of how you will move forward, adopting coping strategies that work for you. Let's consider some examples of coping strategies you could adopt.

Problem-focused strategies

We will start by looking at problem-solving strategies. Here, you are trying to work out a plan for how you would go about solving a specific problem situation, followed by decision-making about which potential solution you would choose. You then should be able to follow through and solve your problem.

Let's consider an example of this process.

Example of a problem-solving strategy
What is the problem? Clearly define the problem you are facing. *My former partner is either driving past where I am living or parking across the street from the house with the intention of intimidating me.*

Generate as many possible solutions as you can. List the ones that are likely to work.
 	
I could do the following:
 	
    I could do nothing and hope he goes away.
 	
    I could contact him and ask him to stay away from my home.
 	
    I could go and stay with friends or family until things blow over.
 	
    I could seek a restraining order, preventing him from coming near my home or me.

Consider the likelihood of each of these strategies being successful. *The likely outcomes are:* *If I did nothing, I doubt things would change. Throughout our relationship, he persevered with intimidating behaviours for long periods of time... sometimes months. Also, if he thinks he has gotten away with intimidating me, his behaviour is likely to escalate.* *By contacting him, I would open up a means of dialogue I do not wish to have. In addition, he would learn that what he was doing was hurting me and I was giving him the power to control me and the degree of upset I experience. This is likely to embolden him to act even more intrusively.* *If I go and stay with friends or family, I cannot guarantee that things will blow over. Also, even if he does not know where I am staying, this is really only a temporary solution. I would have to return to my home at some point. Further, I would be concerned that he would find out where I was staying and would then harass my friends or family members, putting them at risk of harm.* *If I sought a restraining order, I could more safely stay in my own home. If he breached the order, I could easily get support from the police. Also, by doing this, I would demonstrate that I am now willing to stand up to him, letting him know I will no longer tolerate his scare tactics.*

Select the problem-solving strategy that is likely to work the best.
I think I will seek a restraining order. I have enough evidence of his abuse, and I have photographic evidence of his current harassment, so I feel that there is a good likelihood that I will be successful. This is likely to send a strong message that I will not passively tolerate his behaviour any longer.
What are you going to do next?
I will access the application form for a restraining order online. I will complete the application and submit it to the court as soon as possible. I will seek legal advice and support to obtain the order if needed.

In this example, the person has thought about the problem and identified possible options for resolving it. She then considered the likely outcome for each potential solution. She then chose her preferred solution and worked out a plan for her next step. This is a good problem-solving approach.

Here is a problem-solving worksheet you can use.

Problem-solving strategy worksheet
What is the problem? Clearly define the problem you are facing.
Generate as many possible solutions as you can. List the ones that are likely to work.
Consider the likelihood of each of these strategies being successful.
Select the problem-solving strategy that is likely to work the best.

What are you going to do next?

Worksheet available at elemen.com.au

Now, let's consider a cognitive restructuring approach to coping. Cognitive restructuring refers to changing the way you think about a problem. Below is an example of a cognitive restructuring approach to addressing a problem situation.

Example of a cognitive restructuring strategy
What is the problem? *My former partner sent me a message saying that he intended to take the children from me and have them live with him. He said he would see me in court. So, my problem is that he is going to the Family Court to apply for the children to be in his care.*
What are you thinking? *I am going to lose my children. They will end up living with their abusive father, and he will take his anger out on them. I won't be able to protect them.*
What evidence do you have that this is true? *Well... he said he was going to do this, but I guess that isn't evidence it will happen.*
What evidence do you have against this being true? *He has a long history of claiming he was going to do things that he did not end up doing. He does not have the financial means to do this, and he has shown no indication of actually wanting the children in his care.*
Even if it was true, what is the worst thing that would happen? *Even if he did make an application to the Family Court, I have ample evidence of his abuse and the danger he presents to the children to make a strong case for the children remaining in my care. I have many people who support me and know of his behaviour, including his parents and sister. He has a police record, and his abusive behaviour is known to the police, the courts and child protective services. So, the worst thing that would happen is likely to be having to go through a legal process, but there is every indication the children would remain with me.*

What is your conclusion?

I believe this is just another attempt to intimidate me and make me feel fearful. I think I can successfully deal with this if he does make an application to the Family Court, but in the meantime, I think I will focus on other things I can do something about.

Here, the person in this example challenged the way she was thinking about her situation. She examined whether the situation was as bad as she interpreted it. Having realised that was not the case, she worked out a better and more realistic way of thinking about her problem. You can see that her alternative thoughts about her situation would make it easier for her to cope. She had been tormented by thoughts that the children would be taken away from her. Instead, by working through the situation, she could see that she had overreacted to the type of intimidating behaviour her former partner typically used to upset her.

Below is a worksheet you can use to consider a cognitive restructuring coping strategy.

Cognitive restructuring strategy worksheet
What is the problem?
What am I thinking?
What evidence do I have that this is true?
What evidence do I have against this being true?
Even if it was true, what is the worst thing that would happen?

What is my conclusion?

Worksheet available at elemen.com.au

Emotion-focused strategies

Next, we will consider how to enhance your emotion expression coping skills.

Example of an emotion expression strategy
What is the problem?   *I don't want people to know how badly my former partner abused me.*
What did I do?   *I chose not to tell my family about what had happened to me or how I was feeling, and I tried to cope on my own.*
What were the advantages of doing this?   *None, really. I suppose I am protecting my privacy, but it doesn't seem to be working.*
What were the disadvantages of doing this?   *I couldn't talk about how I felt even when I wanted to. I couldn't speak to someone and just let my bottled-up feelings go. I have been pretending everything is okay, which has been really hard, hiding how I feel. There have been times when I have felt so anxious I didn't think I could cope, and there was no one to turn to for help.*
What could I have done differently?   *I could have told my family what had happened, but told them there might have been times when I wanted to talk about it and times when I didn't.*
What would the advantages have been of doing things this other way?   *I would have felt relieved that I wasn't carrying around this huge secret. I would have had family available to talk to about how I was feeling when things were too much for me to cope with. This would have allowed me the opportunity to express how I was feeling in a genuine way. I could have gotten the sympathy and understanding that I needed. My family would have found ways to help me.*

Would there have been any disadvantage of doing things this other way?   *Not really. People would know about my relationship, but now that wouldn't be a disadvantage because it would allow me to openly talk about how I was feeling.*
What will I do next time I feel like this?   *I will sit my family down and tell them what has happened and why I feel so anxious. I will ask for their support, which I know I will receive. I will call them when I feel anxious and need to talk about how I am feeling.*

In this case, the person examined the pros and cons of her decision not to tell anyone about what happened during their relationship. She recognised that this had prevented her from genuinely expressing her emotions in a way that would have been a relief for her. The conclusion was reached that the better option was to allow herself to react in a genuine way to what she was feeling by telling people what had happened so that she did not have to pretend to be all right when she did not feel that way.

Below is a worksheet you can use to develop emotion expression coping strategies.

Emotion expression strategy worksheet
What is the problem?
What did I do?
What were the advantages of doing this?
What were the disadvantages of doing this?

What could I have done differently?
What would the advantages have been of doing things this other way?
Would there have been any disadvantages of doing things this other way?
What will I do next time I feel like this?

Worksheet available at elemen.com.au

Finally, we can consider how to use social support as a coping strategy.

Example of social support as a strategy
What is the problem?   *There have been times when I have felt so anxious that I believed I could not look after myself properly. I felt I couldn't make important decisions because I felt so anxious. There have been many times when I couldn't do normal daily things like shopping and cooking for myself.*
What have I done in response to this problem?   *I just hid out at home and ignored my needs. I have just suffered by myself.*
How has responding in this way helped me with my problem?   *It hasn't helped at all. The decisions I have to make don't get made. My shopping doesn't get done. I don't eat.*

What could I do instead? *I could ask my family to help me. I could ask them to help me work through the decisions I have to make. I could ask them to help me look after myself until I can do it myself.*
How would this be likely to work out? *I know my family would rush to help. I trust their advice, and I believe they can help me with the decisions I have to make. I know they would look after me if they knew I needed them to do that.*
So, what am I going to do next? *Next time I feel like I can't cope, I will pick up the phone and call my family. I will tell them how badly I am feeling and ask them to come to my assistance.*

Here, the person thought through her situation and realised she was doing the opposite of what she should have done to fix her problems. She realised the solution was available to her and that pursuing it had advantages. It was then easy to follow through with her plan and reach out to others.

Below is a worksheet for you to use with a social support coping strategy.

Social support strategy worksheet
What is the problem?
What have I done in response to this problem?
What could I do instead?
How would this be likely to work out?
So, what am I going to do next?

Worksheet available at elemen.com.au

In moving forward, remember to choose the coping strategies that best suit your preferred coping style. No matter your coping style, always choose approach rather than avoidance strategies.

Fix your thinking

It is a fact that how we think affects how we feel and the choices we make regarding our behaviour. Also, it is a fact that experiences such as an abusive relationship can influence the way we think, leading to us making errors in our thinking. You are going to learn more about your thinking, and we will teach you to challenge those errors in thinking so that you can feel better and behave differently.

How are our thoughts affected?

As we go through life, we can develop unhelpful thinking styles or errors in our thinking. These errors influence how we interpret the world around us and how we fit into that world. To make sense of the world, we develop 'templates' or models of how we think things should work or do work.

For example, you might develop a template that tells you that to be a worthwhile person, everyone should like you. On the surface, this seems workable. It is nice when people like you and it makes you feel good, including feeling good about yourself. However, if you have a template that you are worthwhile *only* if everyone likes you, what happens if, for some reason, someone chooses not to like you? You then become upset about something that really is an ordinary enough experience. You then feel like you are not worthwhile, even in situations where the fact that the other person does not like you says more about them than it does about you. We have found that people choose not to like others for the oddest reasons. For example, one person disclosed that they could not like people who vaguely resembled a cousin they did not admire. Should your feelings of self-worth be affected by the fact that you look somewhat like someone you have never met? It is obvious that the answer is no. Unfortunately, your template might tell you that to be a worthwhile person, *everyone* has to like you and here is someone who does not like you. You can see the problem.

Our individual templates are put together based on information from a variety of sources, including, for example, our personality and our experiences throughout life. If the messages we receive from our experiences in life are good and healthy ones, we tend to have good and healthy templates of how the world works and how we fit into that world. However, if the messages are distorted in some way (e.g., being told you have to be the best at everything you do, that no one will like you if you disagree with them, your needs are not as important as other people's needs), then the template we develop will reflect these messages and will be unhelpful.

Core beliefs

So, how does this template affect us? It tells us how we should respond when dealing with our world and the people in it. The information we gather determines our 'core beliefs' about three things:

> How safe or dangerous we perceive the world to be.
>
> Our place in that world and our value as a person.
>
> How certain the future feels.

These core beliefs are not the 'truth' of things. They develop due to the information we gather along the way in life, whether or not that information is helpful or unhelpful, clear or confusing, or accurate or distorted.

If we have helpful, clear, and accurate templates, our core beliefs are healthy, and our thinking does not contain errors about how the world works and how we fit into it. However, if we have unhelpful, confusing, and distorted templates, our thinking contains errors that affect how we react to the world and how we view ourselves in that world.

Cognitive errors

Cognitive errors occur when our templates of how the world works and how we fit into that world send us the wrong message. The wrong message then alters our thinking about our experiences. For example, if an abusive partner repeatedly tells you that you are worthless, your thinking changes so that you come to believe you have no value as a person.

Problems arise when we engage in certain types of cognitive errors. Below are some of the most common cognitive errors. As you read through them, think about whether these types of errors occur in your thinking.

Table 7: Descriptions of the common errors in thinking.

Types of errors in thinking	
Error type	*Error in thinking*
Filtering	A person whose thinking is affected by filtering takes the negative details of an event and exaggerates them while filtering out any positive aspects of the situation. For example, an abused person may focus on a mistake they made that resulted in criticism from their abusive partner, ignoring all the times they did not make a mistake and all the times others had been happy with what they had done in various ways.

Polarised thinking	With polarised thinking, things are either 'black or white' or 'all or nothing'. People who think this way place situations in 'either/or' categories, with no middle ground to account for the complexity of most situations. For example, an abused person may come to believe that either they are a good partner who can make their abuser happy or they are a terrible partner who no one would ever want.
Overgeneralisation	A person makes a conclusion based on one event or a single piece of information. In this way, if something bad happens to them on one occasion, they expect it to happen over and over again. For example, an abused person may believe that because they made a poor choice of partner once, they will make similarly poor choices again and again in the future.
Jumping to conclusions	If a person jumps to conclusions, they 'know' what the other person is thinking about without that person saying so. For example, an abused person may think others think she should have been able to handle the abuse despite them never saying such a thing.
Catastrophising	A person who catastrophises expects disaster to strike, no matter what. A person hears about a problem and uses *what-if* questions to imagine the worst outcome. For example, an abused person may believe that everyone will turn against them if she discloses the abuse she experienced.
Personalisation	A person believes that everything others do or say is some direct, personal reaction to them. They take everything personally. For example, an abused person may believe that the abuser only behaved in an abusive manner because of their own shortcomings and not because the abuser had problems.
Control fallacies	This occurs when a person strongly endorses the view that they must be in control of all situations. This can occur in two ways. Firstly, there is external control, where the person feels they are a helpless victim of fate, and secondly, internal control, where a person assumes responsibility for the pain and unhappiness of others. For example, an abused person may believe that they have triggered the abusive behaviour in their former partner and that the abuse was their fault as a consequence.

Fallacy of fairness	A person who believes they know what is fair will feel resentful and unhappy if others disagree with them. People who judge every event in their lives in terms of whether or not it is fair will often feel resentful, angry and hopeless. For example, an abused person may think that the world is unfair because they have had to endure the abuse rather than seeing that a person's poor behaviour is unrelated to any concept of a 'fair' world.
Blaming	This person holds other people responsible for their own emotional pain. Alternatively, they may blame themselves for every problem – even those clearly outside their control. For example, despite the abuse they endured being related to the abuser's behaviour choices and problems, the abused person will blame herself for the abusive episodes.
Shoulds	Should statements (e.g., I should visit my parents more) are made by people who hold rigid rules about how the world should work and how everyone should behave. Breaking these rules makes a person angry. They also feel guilty when they violate their own rules. For example, the most common manifestations of this error in thinking among abused people are the belief that they should have known from the outset that their partner was abusive and the belief that they should have done something differently to prevent the abuse.
Emotional reasoning	People with this distortion of thinking are guided by what they 'feel' is the truth. They will rely on their feelings to establish whether or not something is 'fact'. If a person feels stupid and boring, they must be stupid and boring. Emotional reasoning blocks rationality and logic. For example, an abused person may feel worthless and of little value, so they believe they are worthless and of little value.
Fallacy of change	A person with this type of thinking will believe that if they apply enough pressure, others will change to meet their needs. This person needs others to change because they cannot cope if others disagree with them or behave in ways that are contrary to how this person feels they should behave. For example, an abused person may believe that if they tried hard enough, they could have changed their partner and turned them into a non-abusive person.

Global labelling	A person generalises a small number of features or characteristics of themselves or others and inflates them into a global statement or judgment. This goes beyond overgeneralising. Rather than take into account the context of a situation, the person will apply this judgment to all aspects of a person or situation. For example, an abused person may come to view themselves as unworthy of love and unworthy of respectful treatment because they have experienced one abusive relationship.
Always being right	When a person engages in this error of thinking, they insist that all views held by them or actions done by them are correct. In their view, they cannot make a mistake or be misinformed. For example, an abused person may disbelieve supporters' acts of support or statements of sympathy and will push these people away to prove they are right that even well-meaning people are untrustworthy.
Heaven's reward fallacy	A person who engages in this type of thinking believes that a person's hard work and sacrifice will pay off in the end, as if someone is keeping track of what everyone does in life. Sharing some similarities with the fallacy of fairness thinking, this person believes that the one who does the most or, works the hardest or sacrifices the most will be the person who is rewarded at some point in the future. For example, throughout an abusive relationship, an abused person may think that if they just do the right thing, put up with the abuse and do everything they can to make the relationship work, it will pay off in the end, and their partner will change into a better person.

Let's consider how these errors in thinking affect a person's point of view. Below are examples of these types of logical errors in thinking, along with a more rational point of view.

Table 8: Examples of rational and irrational perspectives for each error in thinking.

Correcting your thinking	
Error in thinking	*A rational view*
Filtering	
Joanne's family and friends told her she was doing a good job getting her life back on track. They pointed out that she was doing better than they believed they would do in similar circumstances. One person close to Joanne also said that she was 'crazy' to have stayed in an abusive relationship for so long. Joanne only focused on this one negative comment. She concluded that all people viewed her as crazy. This made Joanne feel disheartened.	In general, Joanne should be reassured that people understood her struggles well enough to see that the progress she was making in getting her life back on track was good. She could choose to understand the 'crazy' comment as a reflection of that person's understanding of the severity of the abuse she endured and how difficult it must have been for her. It would have been appropriate for Joanne to consider what people were saying to her and conclude that they genuinely thought she was doing a good job in getting her life back on track.
Polarised thinking	
In an effort to move on with her life, Lily studied at her local college. Overall, she was doing well with her administrative skills course. However, she failed to understand one assignment and received a poor mark. Lily formed the view that, because of her poor mark, she would never get to work in administration. In her mind, she either had to do well on all her assignments or she was going to be a complete failure... as was predicted on many occasions by her former abusive partner.	Lily should have considered her poor mark in the context of her overall performance. In reality, one poor mark is unlikely to affect her overall achievement. In any case, Lily was able to identify why she had obtained the poor mark in that she misunderstood the goal of the assignment. In no way was the one poor mark consistent with her former partner's nasty predictions about her failure in the future. Indeed, when given her next assignment, all Lily has to do is carefully consider what is being asked of her in the assignment and ask for clarification if needed if she wishes to avoid making the same mistake again.

Overgeneralisation	
After the end of her abusive relationship, Sophia met a nice man, Mark, and a relationship was starting to develop. Mark became stressed because of some things that happened at work and was more irritable than usual. Mark snapped at Sophia because of a minor thing she did that annoyed him in his irritated state. Sophia became upset, and Mark became frustrated, so a small argument developed. Sophia formed the view that this relationship with Mark would not work because they had failed to communicate well on this one occasion. She believed that this argument could only lead to the same type of toxic and abusive relationship as the one she had previously endured. Sophia ended the relationship with Mark, seeing no point in trying to work things out.	Sophia would have been better off considering the one minor incident in the context of her other experiences with Mark. Rather than this one argument reflecting an overall pattern of dysfunction in the relationship and a replay of the past abusive relationship, Sophia could have formed the view that this demonstrated nothing more than the fact that people become more irritable if they have had a bad day. Sophia could have understood that expressing irritability is not evidence of the type of abuse she had previously suffered.
Jumping to conclusions	
In her previous relationship, Rebecca had been on the receiving end of abuse on occasions when she made a mistake, had forgotten to do something or had failed to do it to her former partner's satisfaction. The abuse at these times was severe, and now, making mistakes tended to make Rebecca feel anxious. Rebecca made a small error at work, and even though her boss was unconcerned and brushed it off, she was sure that her boss thought she was a hopeless individual who could not do her job properly. Rebecca began to worry that she was going to lose her job. She thought her boss was just waiting for a chance to get rid of her.	Rather than jumping to the worst-case scenario, Rebecca would have felt better if she had been able to focus on the objective facts. Although she was concerned about the error she made, her boss did not agree. In rejecting what her boss told her, she failed to take into account that her boss would be unlikely to dismiss any criticisms of Rebecca's performance if he had genuine concern. Rebecca's anxiety about making mistakes created her worry, not any objective sign that her boss was dissatisfied.

Catastrophising	
Patricia had ignored her parents' repeated requests for her to leave her abusive partner. She had rejected the support her sister had offered her. Although she eventually left the relationship, she had not been ready to do so when her family had encouraged her to leave. Patricia had not been in touch with her family since her relationship with her abusive partner ended. She thought her parents and sister would never forgive her for refusing their advice. She believed they would never speak to her again. Despite her finally having done what her family had wanted her to do and despite knowing they were loving people, Patricia believed that their rejection of her was inevitable.	Patricia formed a view about what would happen due to her disregard of the advice given by her parents and her sister. This view was inconsistent with what she knew about her family members. Given that she knew her parents and sister to be loving and caring people, the chances they would reject Patricia were slim. Patricia was reacting to her own emotional response to her failure to listen to her parents rather than predicting a likely future. In any case, Patricia would not know how her parents and sister would respond to the news that she had left the abusive relationship until she spoke with them about the matter. Predicting a terrible future does not increase the chances that a terrible future will happen, especially if the prediction is based only on fears and not on other information, such as the loving nature of her family members, that Patricia knows to be true.
Personalisation	
Julia's best friend, who had stuck by her throughout her difficult and abusive relationship, had not been in touch for a couple of weeks. Julia was aware that her friend's mother had been very ill and was in hospital. Julia worried that her friend had abandoned her because Julia had recently disclosed to her friend the seriousness of the abuse she had experienced.	In reality, it seems that Julia's friend had a lot on her plate to deal with. It is unlikely, then, that her failure to be in touch was due to Julia disclosing the seriousness of the abuse she experienced. Sometimes, the simplest explanation is the best one. In all likelihood, Julia's friend was busy caring for her mother, and her failure to get in touch had nothing to do with Julia.

Control fallacies	
Andrea had had two significant relationships in her life. The first began when she was quite young and lasted for several years. The relationship was unstable as they both grew into adulthood. The second relationship was the abusive one that was very difficult for Andrea and caused her much distress. Andrea formed the view that she was unlucky in relationships and that there was nothing she could do about this. She felt she was doomed to repeat bad experiences in the future, no matter with whom she formed a relationship. As a result, Andrea thought she should avoid relationships in the future.	Andrea has fallen into the trap of believing that two unhappy experiences indicated control by some force she labelled as 'poor luck'. She could realise that both relationships had failed for very different reasons. She could also realise that the choices she makes about future relationships are hers, and the wisdom she has gained from bad experiences will help her avoid similar experiences in the future. Thinking in this better way, Andrea could understand that it is not necessary to face a future alone.

Fallacy of fairness	
The more Jacqueline thought about it, the more she thought it was unfair that she had had to endure the abuse she experienced in her relationship. She told herself that others did not have to put up with that sort of treatment, and it was unfair that she had to do so. She thought about what she had done for her partner and how she had treated him well. She thought it was not fair that she had been on the receiving end of the abuse, given that she would never have behaved like that to him. Jacqueline was driving herself crazy thinking about all the ways the world had been unfair to her. She was overwhelmed by anger and resentment.	It is a fact that, despite our best efforts, things do not always work out the way we want. Bad things can happen to anyone. Jacqueline would be better off thinking that the world is neither fair nor unfair. Individuals are in charge of how they choose to conduct themselves. It was disappointing that Jacqueline's ex-partner chose to behave aggressively and that he chose not to seek help for his anger management problems. However, his decisions did not indicate an unfair world.

Blaming	
Ava has been struggling since the end of her abusive relationship. She has been wondering whether it was the right thing to do to leave the relationship. In the few weeks since she left, she has found it difficult to establish a life for herself. Ava has been blaming herself for the problems in the relationship despite her being the target of her ex-partner's abusive behaviour. She has been going over in her mind times when she now thinks she should have tried harder to please her partner or not done things that seemed to aggravate him. She keeps thinking she is the one to blame for the difficulties she experienced.	It seems that Ava is blaming herself for her partner's abuse of her and the need to end the relationship primarily because she is struggling to cope in the aftermath of the end of the relationship. It would be better for Ava to understand her current difficulties as a result of the unwarranted abuses she endured. She had little choice but to leave the relationship if her long-term well-being was important to her. Certainly, her reasons for leaving were legitimate. Blaming herself because she is currently unhappy does not alter the fact that abuse of a partner is unwarranted and an act of violence, no matter its form. She was justified in leaving for that reason and because to stay would only have meant that she would have experienced more abuse.
Shoulds	
Beth thought she should have been doing better than she is currently. She recently left an abusive relationship, and she expected that things should have immediately improved. She thought that she should have looked for work by now and that she should have socialised more with friends now that she is single. Beth is confused by her current situation. She is feeling intensely anxious much of the time but still believes she should be doing better and doing more than she is doing. She is disregarding the psychological impact of her relationship experiences.	Often, the demands we place on ourselves increase the pressure we feel. In reality, rather than demanding of herself that she do better, Beth would be better off choosing to do what is necessary for her to manage her anxiety and feel more settled before trying to achieve more challenging goals she might set for herself. Despite the demands we place on ourselves with thoughts like "I should…" and "I must…" much of what we choose to do or not do reflects our preferences. Beth would be better off choosing to look after her mental health as a priority.

Emotional reasoning	
After the abusive relationship she endured, Suzanne reached the conclusion that she would never be in a relationship again because she was unlovable. She felt she had no redeeming qualities that would attract a partner. She believed she was going to be alone forever. The abuse Suzanne had experienced altered the way she thought about herself. Although previously secure, self-sufficient and well-adjusted, Suzanne understood she had changed because of the abuse. She now felt diminished by her experiences, unworthy and valueless.	Suzanne's strong emotional reaction to the abuse has caused her to believe that her views about her future are the 'truth'. Despite having no evidence that she will never find someone who would love her, she strongly believes this to be true only because she feels badly about herself. She has got this the wrong way around. At the moment, she is saying to herself, "Because I feel bad, the thing I fear is true". She would be better off exploring relationship opportunities when she is ready and then determining whether all this worry is necessary.
Fallacy of change	
Eloise has a friend who experienced abuse in a relationship that was similar to the abuse Eloise had experienced. Eloise thought she had found someone who could truly understand what she had been going through. However, Eloise's friend was never very comfortable talking about her feelings. In contrast, Eloise was more able to talk about her emotional reactions to what had happened to her. Eloise kept contacting her friend to talk about their similar experiences. Eloise thought her friend needed to open up and talk more about how she was feeling. She was disappointed and upset when her friend kept rejecting her efforts to meet for a discussion.	Eloise has mistakenly assumed that because she values something, everyone else should also value it. Eloise is expecting her friend to change to meet her needs. Eloise is upset because she believes her friend is deliberately withholding something from her that she strongly wants. She fails to see that she is upsetting herself by expecting her friend to change and offer Eloise something her friend cannot provide. Eloise would feel less stressed if she could accept that people cannot be expected to change to meet her needs and look for support elsewhere.

Global labelling	
Amelia is convinced she is hopeless and will fail at everything she tries to undertake. Amelia formed this view as a result of the abusive relationship she experienced. Her abusive boyfriend had repeatedly made comments about her worthlessness. He blamed her for his abusive behaviour, claiming Amelia had failed to be the sort of person he was looking for. Amelia formed the view that she just was not good enough and could not do anything right. She believed she would repeatedly fail so there was no point in trying.	Amelia's upset emotional state is colouring the way she views herself in a global sense. One relationship did not work out, and her abusive partner blamed her, so Amelia decided that everything about her was terrible and she would fail at everything she undertook. The leap from the comments made by an abusive partner to a belief that she would never be able to do otherwise was illogical. She would have been better off seeing that one abusive person's views had no bearing on her successes in a future that did not even involve him.
Always being right	
Catherine realised she was a changed person because of her ex-partner's abusive behaviour towards her. Her former partner was the sort of person who refused to let go of anything and always insisted he was right and, therefore, Catherine was wrong. Intense arguments would develop over minor matters because of his insistence on winning every argument. If she had tried to escape from these interactions, her ex-partner would follow her, demanding that she acknowledge he was right. Catherine had been exhausted by these interactions. However, he had been so insistent that he was right that Catherine has questioned her own point of view.	Catherine's ex-partner had caused problems by his insistence that the only acceptable outcome of an argument was for him to be 'proven' right. He refused to accept or understand that other people might hold an opinion different to his own. He was unable to feel all right if others disagreed with him. He could not understand that he could be all right if others saw things from a different perspective. He used his force of will to bring Catherine into line. This made Catherine confused and unhappy. Now, Catherine needed to learn to see her ex-partner's behaviour in the context of the errors he was making in his thinking.

Heaven's reward fallacy	
Despite the abuse she experienced from her former partner, prior to their break-up, Odette had always put her partner's needs before her own. She ran around after him, she listened to his problems and tried to help, she did all the housework and got him out of financial difficulties he had caused on numerous occasions. However, when she developed a problem of her own, Odette was surprised that her ex-partner had been unwilling to do anything to help her. Despite all the effort she put into helping him, he refused to reciprocate. Her ex-partner's failure to help her when she really needed assistance had hurt and confused Odette. She thought she had done enough to earn some support from him.	Odette had mistakenly believed that because she had done the right thing, her partner would do the same. Everyone is driven by their own motivations. Each person sets a standard for their own behaviour. Although it would be nice if others reciprocated, there is no guarantee that will happen when you enter into a relationship of any sort with another person.

It is apparent that these types of logical errors do not make things easy for us. Quite the opposite. They lead us to misinterpret events so that we adopt a limited or negative perspective that colours how we view things, our emotional responses, and the choices of how we behave.

Why do we think in unhelpful ways?

Why do we think in ways that are distorted and not particularly helpful? To understand why errors in thinking happen, we have to consider the theory behind cognitive behaviour therapy (CBT). According to this theory, our thinking has more than one level. This is displayed in the diagram below.

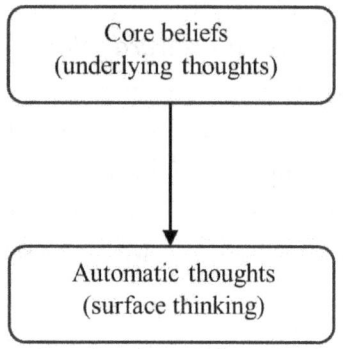

Figure 5: A diagram of the two levels of thought.

Automatic thoughts refer to the running commentary that goes through our heads as we go about our daily lives. If you pay attention, you will notice the constant chatter in your head about what you are doing and how you are reacting to the people and events around you.

There is an easy exercise that will show you how this running commentary works. For the next minute, think about a bowl of fruit. Over the course of the minute, just let your thoughts do what they want as you think about a bowl of fruit. At the end of the minute, notice where your thoughts have taken you. Now consider the links between your starting point (thinking about a bowl of fruit) and where you ended up (thinking whatever it was you were thinking). Consider below how this might have played out for one individual. This person started thinking about a bowl of fruit and ended up thinking about cleaning out their pantry. Follow their automatic thoughts.

> *Ok. I'm thinking about a bowl of fruit. I can picture a bowl of fruit. It's got bananas in it. I like bananas. I should buy some next time I go to the supermarket. I also need to get a loaf of bread. I must start a shopping list. Pay attention and think about a bowl of fruit. Oh, and milk, I mustn't forget milk. I hate running out of milk. Someone once said they have orange juice on their cereal instead of milk. Yuck. I couldn't imagine anything worse. Not that I eat much cereal. I should eat more cereal… it's probably good for you. I will put cereal on my shopping list. But that might be a waste because I probably won't eat it. I have bought lots of things I thought would be good for me, but I never ate them. That reminds me that I should clean out the pantry.*

In contrast to automatic, surface thoughts, core beliefs refer to the underlying beliefs we have about how the world works and how we fit into that world. Core beliefs influence our automatic thoughts. That is, we think the things we do on the surface because of our underlying beliefs about how things work. Unlike automatic thoughts, the content of our core beliefs is not readily available to us but can be examined by considering the content of our automatic thoughts.

So, where do the logical errors in thinking we have been talking about fit into this conceptualisation? Let's consider that in the diagram below.

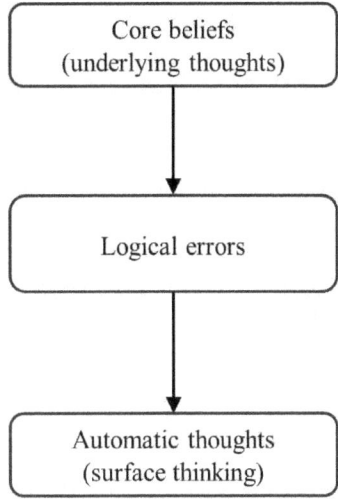

Figure 6: Where errors in thinking occur in our levels of thought.

The errors in thinking we make are a result of the core beliefs we hold. For example, if our core beliefs about the world and the future are that the world is threatening and the outlook is grim and pessimistic, then we are likely to inflate the degree of dangerousness we perceive, and we are likely to catastrophise.

These logical errors then affect our surface thinking. Because of the logical errors we make based on our particular core beliefs, we are more likely to be self-critical, tell ourselves everything is hopeless, or say nothing is fair. Logical errors are inevitable if there are problems with our core beliefs.

Our core beliefs are built based on a variety of influences. These include our genetic makeup (e.g., an inherited overly reactive nervous system), our experiences (the things that happen to us), the messages we receive (the things people have said to us or the way they have treated us), and the ways we have interpreted these events. If the influences are positive and healthy, our core beliefs tend to be clear, and logical errors are few. If the influences on us are negative, unhealthy or confusing, our core beliefs tend to be inaccurate, and the logical errors we make are many, and they strongly influence our automatic thoughts.

Underlying assumptions of logical errors

It has been suggested that each logical error is driven by specific assumptions. If our automatic thoughts are biased, then the biases are driven by our core beliefs and assumptions. Below are some examples of cognitive errors and associated assumptions. Here, we are referring to the assumptions that are inevitably made if the errors in our thinking are present.

Table 9: The assumptions underlying each logical error.

Cognitive error	Assumption
Filtering	The only events that matter are failures. I should measure myself by my errors.
Polarised thinking	Everything is always one extreme or the other.
Overgeneralisation	If it's true in one case, it must be true in every case that is even slightly similar.
Jumping to conclusions	If it has always been true in the past, it is going to be true in the future.
Catastrophising	Always think the worst because it is most likely to happen to you.
Personalisation	I am responsible for all bad things, failures, etc.
Control fallacies	You should be able to know in advance what is going to happen. You should have seen the bad thing coming before it happened.
Fallacy of fairness	The world is a fair place and fairness will influence how things turn out.
Blaming	Whether it is me or someone else, someone is always responsible when things are not the way I want them to be.
Shoulds	People have an obligation to do specific things that cannot be avoided.
Emotional reasoning	If a person feels bad, something must be wrong.
Fallacy of change	People must change to meet other people's needs.
Global labelling	A whole person and their entire life can be summed up by a single word (e.g., stupid).

Always being right	People have to choose a side, and there is a right side and a wrong side.
Heaven's reward fallacy	Choosing to do good things for others will oblige others to do good things in return.

Let's consider how these logical errors and the assumptions that are made affect automatic thoughts. Consider in this example what this person is saying to herself about her relationship breakdown.

> *My head is spinning. I can't believe the relationship is over. It was a terrible time. I don't even know what went wrong, but I must have done something… or not done something to cause this to happen* (personalisation). *I am always so hopeless, and I'm never good enough* (global labelling). *It serves me right. I deserve to be in this mess* (blaming). *I should have seen it coming from the moment I met him and got out of there before things got this bad* (control fallacy).

Let's break this down and see where this person is making mistakes.

> Despite having been on the receiving end of the abuse in the relationship, she has assumed that she is the one responsible – that there was something she could have done differently to achieve a better outcome (personalisation). It seems unreasonable for her to hold this view.

> As a result of her version of her contribution to the relationship failing, she is self-critical and attributes certain characteristics to herself that attack her, not just in terms of the relationship problem, but in all things (global labelling). Even if she did make mistakes in her relationship, it does not follow that she is a bad or hopeless person deserving of bad things happening to her.

> Then, even though it was her partner who abused her in the relationship, she holds herself responsible and thinks she deserves what she has experienced (blaming). She is pointing the finger at herself despite having no evidence that she is the one who should be held accountable.

> Finally, even though she could not have controlled what happened, she believes she should have known in advance what was to come and then acted even before the abuse began (control fallacy). This suggests that she should have magically known in advance what was going to happen and she could have and should have controlled the end result.

The errors in this person's thinking have resulted in her feeling much worse than she would have if she had not made these errors. Let's find out how to change this way of thinking to protect yourself from the negative effects of logical errors.

Understanding automatic thoughts

The goal here is to teach you to think in a more realistic and balanced way so that you can cope better in the aftermath of the end of the abusive relationship. Let's begin this process.

Everybody experiences automatic thoughts. They reflect our way of making sense of and reacting to the world around us and to internal experiences, such as anxiety or memories and urges. Automatic thoughts are often highly believable, even when they are based on logical errors. As a result of their believability, we tend not to challenge them. If they pass unchallenged, they can have a profound and detrimental effect on our emotional state. For example, if a person thinks they are stupid and they do not challenge that thought, they are likely to feel upset and unworthy.

Consider this example.

> *"This must have been my fault. If only I could have been a better partner, maybe none of this would have happened. He kept telling me I didn't do the right thing… that I couldn't do anything right. Maybe if I had tried harder, things would have been better."*

It would be hard to think this way without feeling bad as a consequence. We tend to believe the things we tell ourselves. Even when we do not pay much attention to our self-talk – our running commentary – we can still be affected by it.

Catching automatic thoughts

It is important to pay attention to your automatic thoughts so that their content can be used to identify the logical errors you are making and, ultimately, your core beliefs. The way to go about this is to keep a thought record related to times when you notice a change in the way you are feeling.

In its simplest form, a thought record asks you to identify the event that has occurred, to take notice of the thoughts that go through your head at the time of the event, and to record the consequences you experience, both in terms of how you feel and how you might act in response. Consider the example below of a simple thought record.

A	B	C
Activating event	Belief or thought	Consequence: emotional and behavioural
Andrew rang me and told me it was my fault that he had to leave me, and now the kids won't have their father.	*I should have tried harder.*	*I felt really upset. I talked to a friend about whether I should forget about the abuse and beg him for forgiveness.*

We do not usually pay much attention to the thoughts that go through our heads, even though they can have such a profound effect on how we are feeling and what we choose to do as a result of feeling that way. To change our thinking, we have to learn to identify our automatic thoughts. When we consider the events that trigger a response in us, we can usually identify what went through our mind at the time.

By keeping track of your automatic thoughts, you can find patterns in your thinking that are linked with particular negative feelings and the behaviours you choose because you are feeling that way. Use the simple thought record below to keep track of your automatic thoughts about events that stress you.

Simple automatic thoughts worksheet		
A	B	C
Activating event	Belief or thought	Consequence: emotional and behavioural

Worksheet available at elemen.com.au

Understanding and noticing logical errors

Everyone makes logical errors. It is important to understand this point. When the error you are making (e.g., everything should be fair) conflicts with how things really are (e.g., the world is neither fair nor unfair, it just is the way it is), problems arise. However, it is also important to be able to recognise the logical errors you are making so that you can correct them and correct the problems in your core beliefs. To do this, you can try the simple approach of expanding on your thought record form to include the types of logical errors reflected in your automatic thoughts.

Let's go back to our original thought record form and expand the examples.

Expanded thought record form - example			
A	B	C	D
Activating event	Belief or thought	Consequence: emotional and behavioural	Logical errors
Andrew rang me and told me it was my fault that he had to leave me, and now the kids won't have their father.	I should have tried harder and tolerated the abuse.	I felt really upset. I talked to a friend about whether I should forget about the abuse and beg him for forgiveness.	Blaming (self)

This person accepted Andrew's statement and blamed herself for Andrew's decision to leave and the abuse she experienced. She held herself responsible for things that were not in her control.

Below is an expanded thought record form that you can use to identify your logical errors in what you are thinking.

Expanded thought record form - example			
A	B	C	D
Activating event	Belief or thought	Consequence: emotional and behavioural	Logical errors

Worksheet available at elemen.com.au

Reframing your thoughts (cognitive restructuring)

The process of challenging our negative automatic thoughts is called cognitive restructuring. This is what we are trying to achieve here. The conclusions we reach because of our logical errors should be challenged and replaced with something that is healthier and more accurately reflects how the world really works.

Although there are lots of ways you can go about restructuring your thinking, we are going to introduce you to a straightforward method. We are going to start by ensuring that you understand the difference between fact and opinion. This is important as our thoughts and decision-making should be based on facts and not the opinions we form because of incorrect information that can underlie our core beliefs. For example, an opinion would be "I am stupid". You might form this opinion because someone has repeatedly told you that you are stupid or because they acted in a way that encouraged you to believe you were stupid. It is not the truth or a fact that you are stupid, even if you have done unwise things. It is a belief you have or an opinion you have formed because of incorrect information.

We refer to the opinion on which you rely as a work of fiction. That is, you write a story in your head about what is happening and then act as if the story is true. You need to be able to identify when you are relying on the story you have written in your mind rather than basing your thoughts on factual evidence. Let's start by having a go at identifying fact from opinion or fiction. In the spaces provided, you can add other things you have been thinking and consider whether they are facts or opinions.

Fact or fiction worksheet		
Statement	*Fact*	*Fiction*
I am stupid		√
I love bushwalking	√	
I am ugly		
I forgot to renew my driver's licence		
No one likes me		
This will be a disaster		
I'm not good enough		

I am single		
I will never fall in love again		
I hate my job		
I should have known what was about to happen		
There are times when people feel stressed		

Checklist available at elemen.com.au

The facts here are:

    I love bushwalking

    I forgot to renew my driver's licence

    I am single

    I hate my job

    There are times when people feel stressed

The statements that are opinions are:

    I am stupid

    I am ugly

    No one likes me

    This will be a disaster

    I'm not good enough

    I will never fall in love again

    I should have known what was about to happen

Why should we make this distinction between what is a fact and what is an opinion? It is because the errors in thinking we make are based on opinion and not on fact. Further, because we hold this opinion, we assume that it is true because we are thinking it and not because it is based on fact.

To tidy up our thinking and remove the logical errors, we have to rely on those thoughts that are based on fact alone. We can reject thoughts that are just based on our opinion because our opinions can be faulty. Factual information will be a good guide for us to determine whether or not we should believe what we are thinking. Consider the following example.

Cognitive restructuring worksheet
What I am thinking *I am thinking that I should have tried harder and behaved differently so that Andrew would not have been forced to treat me so badly.*
Facts supporting the thought *He might have said I should have tried harder, but that is not a fact.*
Facts contradicting the thought *I did all I could to cope with the abuse.* *I was abused whether or not I had done anything wrong.* *Throughout our relationship, Andrew often blamed me for his wrongdoing.* *Andrew had abused other partners in the past.* *Andrew was not forced to treat me and his other partners in an abusive manner.*
Is this thought based on factual evidence or opinion? *It seems that my thoughts are just based on an opinion. It was an opinion that Andrew expressed, and then I believed him and adopted his opinion. No one is responsible for Andrew's behaviour and decisions except for Andrew.*

By looking at the facts for and against a point of view being true, you can work out the value of holding that opinion. It seems like a waste of time to be thinking a particular thing and being negatively affected by it emotionally and behaviourally if you cannot even determine that the opinion reflects the truth. You can use the worksheet below to examine your thoughts in terms of the facts supporting what you are thinking and the facts that contradict what you are thinking.

Cognitive restructuring worksheet
What I am thinking
Facts supporting the thought
Facts contradicting the thought
Is this thought based on factual evidence or opinion?

Worksheet available at elemen.com.au

Rather than looking at facts for and against the truth of your thoughts, another and very easy approach to reframing your thinking is called compassionate cognitive restructuring. Here, you are asked to look at your thoughts in a more compassionate way. Ask yourself what you would say to a person who is in a similar situation to you. In all likelihood, you would say something much kinder and closer to the truth than you are saying to yourself.

Consider this example.

Example:	
Your friend says:	*He only hit me because I wasn't a good enough partner. He only left because I wasn't good enough.*
You might say:	*That's not true. I know you did all you could to make that relationship work. But the truth is, he is an aggressive person who hits women when things aren't going his way. His decisions to do these things are his. There was nothing you could have done to make it stop. If there was, you would have done it.*

It is the case that we often are harder on ourselves than others think is necessary. We set higher standards. For example, you might say that you should never make a mistake and call yourself stupid if you do. Your friend would say that everyone makes mistakes, and all we can do is learn from them.

Interestingly, although you trust your good friends, you choose not to believe them when they make an honest, positive statement about you. Remember how it feels when the reverse occurs when you make a positive statement to your friend, and they dismiss what you say or reject it in favour of a statement you see as false. It is frustrating. You can be as kind and supportive to yourself as you are to the people you care about.

Making the restructured thinking habitual

To get to a point where you are thinking in a healthier way, you need to go through a process of deliberately challenging your thinking. You need to overlearn to notice your automatic thoughts and then reframe them into healthier, more accurate alternative thoughts. You will then move on to challenging your thinking and adjusting your automatic thoughts without giving it much attention. Eventually, you will not even have to do that because your core beliefs will be corrected to offer you a more accurate template of how the world works and how you fit into that world.

Targeting the assumptions

Let's not forget those assumptions that underlie the errors you make in your thinking. You need to challenge those assumptions to correct your thinking completely. Remember, if the assumptions that underlie the error are shown to be wrong, there is every reason to abandon the logical error and replace it with a more logical point of view.

There are a few ways you can challenge the assumptions that underlie logical errors. We are going to focus on three approaches. Firstly, we are going to apply the strategy of looking at the advantages and disadvantages of holding an assumption. Consider the following example of someone who is predicting that things are going to work out poorly.

Assumption worksheet: Advantages and disadvantages
Logical error and assumption *Catastrophising. Always think the worse because it is most likely going to happen to you.*
Advantages *I will always be on 'red alert' in case something happens.*
Disadvantages *I will be on 'red alert' all the time, even when it is not necessary for me to be so.* *I will find it hard to feel any joy about anything if I constantly worry about everything going wrong.* *I will waste a lot of time worrying about things that end up not being as bad as I thought they were going to be.*

Challenging the assumption that underlies a tendency to catastrophise, you can see that there are many more disadvantages to doing this than there are advantages. In fact, experiencing the disadvantages may turn out to be worse than the possible thing in the future you are worrying about.

Secondly, you can act against the assumptions. What would happen if the assumption was incorrect? Consider the following example.

Assumption worksheet: Acting against the assumption
Logical error and assumption *Catastrophising. Always think the worst because it is most likely going to happen to you.*
Things that might happen if I acted like the assumption was not true *I might be able to relax and feel calmer.* *I might find some enjoyment in the things I do.* *I might experience some peace of mind.* *I might look forward to some things in the future.*

By acting as if the assumption is false, you can usually identify the positive things that would occur as a consequence. All of these things are better than predicting a gloomy future. Remember, spending your time thinking about how badly things are likely to turn out in the future also removes all the pleasure from the present.

Finally, you can argue against the assumption. You can take the perspective that the assumption is wrong and develop an argument for your case. Consider the following example.

Assumption worksheet: Arguing against the assumption
Logical error and assumption *Catastrophising. Always think the worse because it is most likely to happen to you.*
Arguments against the assumption *Thinking something might happen will not make it happen.* *There is no cosmic force that is directing all bad things my way.*

Here, you are thinking of the *facts* that can be used to present a good argument that the assumption associated with the logical error is not accurate. This will allow you to challenge your error-ridden thinking and replace it with healthier thinking that will not encourage you to feel strong, negative emotions.

Below is a worksheet you can use to challenge the assumptions that underlie your errors in thinking.

Targeting assumptions worksheet
Logical error and assumption
Advantages
Disadvantages
Things that might happen if I acted like the assumption was not true
Arguments against the assumption

Worksheet available at elemen.com.au

Here, we have asked you to consider challenging the sorts of thoughts you might have that are likely to make you feel worse than you would otherwise feel if you did not think that way. You have learned to access these logical errors by paying attention to your automatic thoughts that serve as the running commentary your mind provides. You have learned ways to challenge these errors and remove them and their influence from your thinking. The goal of doing these things has been to help you manage your distress and to protect yourself from distress in the future. It then becomes important to re-establish some things you have lost as a result of being in an abusive relationship. We will consider these next.

Re-establish a sense of self and self-worth

Your sense of self refers to your perception of who you are and the traits that define you. It allows you to know who you are and guides you in terms of what you stand for. People with a strong sense of self understand their own value even if they sometimes make mistakes or poor decisions.

Self-worth refers to the belief you have in your value as a person. People with high self-worth understand they deserve respect, love and consideration just because of who they are rather than what they have earned. Both your sense of self and your self-worth can be damaged by the experience of relationship abuse.

Factors that enhance a sense of self and self-worth

A variety of factors are associated with your sense of self and your feelings of self-worth. They are the things that can define your sense of self and your understanding of who you are. They are also the things that can be damaged by the experiences you have during a relationship with an abusive partner.

Your personal values

Your values relate to how you understand right from wrong. They are associated with what you choose to stand for. Living up to the standards you set can enhance your sense of self and your self-worth.

Your self-assurance

Self-assurance is associated with a calm sense of acceptance of yourself and a belief in yourself. It implies a certainty of who you are without reliance on other people's perceptions of you or trying to copy other people's identities.

Your interests

Seeking out hobbies and activities that reflect your interests can enhance your self-worth. This is because you are doing things that give you pleasure, provide you with opportunities for achievement and satisfaction, and give you a defined sense of who you are and what you enjoy.

Your emotional stability

The more emotionally stable you feel, the better your self-worth. This is particularly the case if you learn to respond appropriately to self-criticism, rejecting the damaging effects of excessive self-criticism in favour of self-care.

The fulfilment you get from relationships

Here, we are not talking about what others might want in their relationships but what would be fulfilling for you. One factor that will enhance your self-worth is a belief in your worthiness to be loved and to offer love.

Employment

Although career pathways can be stressful and put too much pressure on you, being gainfully employed can be associated with your self-worth. The sense of satisfaction you can gain from being financially self-sufficient and your ability to look after yourself can boost your sense of self and self-worth.

These features can be fundamental to your sense of self-worth and offer opportunities to improve and develop your sense of self-worth. Additionally, there are other ways that you can enhance your self-worth.

How to build self-worth

Develop a support network

A support system of family and friends can act as a buffer against the stress you experience at challenging times in your life. Turning to others for support when you need help is a useful thing to do. The people you turn to can help you build your self-worth by helping you realise how valued you are by these people.

Avoid comparing yourself to others

Do not try to determine where you should be in life by making comparisons between yourself and others. Everyone follows their own path through life, experiencing different things along the way. It is not useful to make unrealistic comparisons that only serve to undermine your self-worth, even though they are based on unreasonable standards you have set for yourself.

Be compassionate with yourself

Unconstructive self-criticism never really helps anyone. Instead, use a strengths-based approach to life, building on what you do well rather than focusing on what you struggle to do well—a deficits-based approach. Be kind to yourself and recognise that you can choose to do more of what you do best rather than criticise yourself for failing to do the things you cannot do.

Consider your role in the lives of other people

Give some thought to the meaning you have for the people you care about in your life. It is not really for you to judge how much you mean to them. It is up to them to decide this. Even if you do not see yourself as worthy, recognise that others may see you as an essential and much-loved person in their lives.

Be inspired by others in a similar situation to you

Try to be like those people you respect. Learn from their experiences. Gain wisdom from what they have been through and successfully managed.

Find a challenge

Take a step outside your comfort zone and undertake a challenge that stretches you. Do something you have not done before. Congratulate yourself on your achievements.

Understand it is not what happens…

The importance here is to develop an understanding that it is not what happens to you that will determine your self-worth but how you respond to what happens to you. That is, experiencing difficult things in life will not determine who you are as a person. You just need to remember that you are responsible for and in control of how you think about a situation and what you choose to do.

You can select your preferred ways of enhancing your self-worth or use all these suggestions. Certainly, there is no one individual thing that will be effective. Rather, it is an accumulation of factors that impact how you view yourself and your worth.

In addition to the things you can do to improve your self-worth, consideration should be given to how you think and the beliefs you hold and their impact on your self-worth. Before moving on, let's consider ways you can think that will have an effect on your view of yourself.

Thoughts and beliefs to promote high self-worth

We know that the way we think can affect how we feel and what we choose to do. Let's consider the types of thoughts that can improve self-worth.

> *"I am worthy of love no matter what I have or have not done in the past."*

Although you need to take responsibility for your actions, you do not need to denigrate yourself for what you have done. Learn from your mistakes and move on.

> *"What I have does not define who I am."*

It is not what or how much you have or own that will determine your self-worth. It is helpful to recognise that 'things' can be impermanent. Things change, accidents happen, and relationships come to an end.

> *"I have the right to feel whatever it is I am feeling."*

To achieve self-worth, you do not have to be happy all the time. That is not what will establish your self-worth. As human beings, we are capable of a full range of emotions, and they all have a purpose. They allow us to express ourselves. It is reasonable to acknowledge and experience our emotions.

> *"There is no reason to be afraid of being alone."*

People with high self-worth will make time for themselves and not fear being left out of things. They are not overly concerned about how other people view them. People invited into their lives will receive that invitation because they have earned the right.

Working on developing your sense of self and your self-worth is a useful undertaking because of the effect that an abusive relationship can have on how you view yourself. However, another important aspect of how we function may need to be re-established. Here, we are referring to self-efficacy.

Re-build your self-efficacy

Self-efficacy refers to your belief that you can do what you set out to do. The word 'efficacy' means 'the ability to produce a desired or intended result'. We are going to consider how the experience of abusive relationships can affect self-efficacy. We will also look at ways to restore self-efficacy.

The concept of self-efficacy

The idea of self-efficacy was initially developed by a Canadian-American psychologist, Albert Bandura. He identified self-efficacy as an important feature of how you think, feel, and motivate yourself. Self-efficacy contributes to:

> How much effort you put into a task
>
> How will you persist with a task
>
> How resilient you are in response to challenges that might prevent you from achieving your goal.

People with high self-efficacy are usually confident in how they approach a task. When faced with obstacles, they view them as able to be overcome. They are also ambitious in their goals. In contrast, people with low self-efficacy tend to doubt their ability to complete a task. They cope poorly with the challenges they might face. They are more likely to give up and not complete a task when confronted with a setback.

Interestingly, self-efficacy can vary across different areas of your life. For example, you may have high self-efficacy concerning your work tasks but low self-efficacy regarding relationships.

The link between self-efficacy and relationship abuse

There are a number of factors that influence your self-efficacy. Importantly, self-efficacy is affected by the experiences you have in life. In this way, relationship abuse can impact your level of self-efficacy. These types of experiences undermine your belief that you can do what you set out to do.

Why is self-efficacy important?

Self-efficacy is important because of its role in how you feel about yourself and whether you can pursue and successfully achieve your life goals. With low self-efficacy, you may not even try to undertake a task or strive for a goal because you simply believe that you cannot achieve what you set out to do. This can significantly limit your life in many ways.

Ways to improve self-efficacy

Here, we have identified things you can do to build your self-efficacy. These straightforward methods will build your confidence in your ability to do what you set out to do.

Set goals that are achievable

Do not set yourself up to fail by setting goals that are too hard to achieve. Instead, set goals that are manageable and achievable. You are better off striving for an easier goal with a greater certainty of success than aiming for a bigger goal that is unlikely to be achieved. The goals you set can be more difficult or challenging as you become more confident in your ability to do what you set out to do. Consider this example.

> *Carla wanted to get a job, but the thought of doing so was overwhelming. She wasn't sure she could do that and be useful to an employer. She decided to take things a step at a time. Carla thought it best to focus on what she had to do to get her life in order, such as dealing with the bank. She thought that when everything was going smoothly, she might undertake a training course and then when she was ready, re-enter the workforce. She felt more confident about doing it this way than jumping in the deep end. She was worried that she would fail if she tried to get a job immediately.*

Break down tasks into smaller, achievable goals

A good approach to building your self-efficacy is to break down your goals into smaller, manageable tasks. By doing this, you are likely to feel less overwhelmed by the enormity of what you are trying to achieve. When you successfully achieve the smaller goals, your confidence in your capacity to do what you set out to do will be enhanced.

> *Kristie had been staying with family since she left the abusive relationship. She knew she had to find a place to live but felt unable to even think about what she would have to do to move into a new home. Kristie's sister helped her break down the task into smaller steps that Kristie could undertake without feeling the task was impossible. They made a list for Kristie to work on. On the list were tasks such as the two sisters visiting various neighbourhoods to see which appealed to Kristie, investigating whether Kristie was entitled to rental assistance from the government, looking on the real estate rental website, and visiting properties with her sister that Kristie was interested in viewing. Approaching each task separately, Kristie felt more confident that she could find somewhere to live.*

Imagine succeeding

We often undermine our success in undertaking a task by predicting failure. Instead, you should picture yourself successfully completing the task and achieving your goal. When you are faced with a particular challenge, imagine what it would be like to go ahead and do what you set out to do.

> *Leah had to go to court to seek a restraining order against her abusive former partner, who had been threatening her since she left the relationship. She dreaded having to do so, imagining herself falling to pieces in court, unable to convey the problems she faced. On the advice of a friend, Leah decided to picture herself in her mind undertaking this task with confidence. She pictured what she would be wearing to improve her confidence, as she walked into the court with her lawyer and took a seat. She imagined herself talking in court and relating what she had been experiencing. She pictured herself speaking clearly and coherently. She imagined what it would be like to be granted the restraining order. She pictured herself walking out of the court with her head held high.*

Look for positive role models

Look for people who you know can successfully do what you want to be able to do. Examine how they go about the task and identify the strategies they use. If you feel comfortable, ask them how they succeed in the tasks they undertake.

> *Maddie's confidence in her ability to follow through and do the things she needed to do had been undermined by her long-term, abusive relationship. Her former partner had repeatedly told her that she was stupid and incapable of doing anything. However, now that Maddie had left the relationship, she knew things had to change. She knew that she had to take charge of her life, no matter how lacking in confidence she felt. So, Maddie decided to ask for advice from her friend, who had been through a similar relationship but had managed to move on and be successful in her life after the end of the relationship. This friend was happy to help Maddie.*

Reflect on successes you have had in the past

Remember when you have been faced with a challenge or undertook a task you no longer feel able to do but have successfully done what you set out to do in the past. Reflect on times when you have faced difficulties and managed to deal with them. Everyone has been successful some of the time.

> *Since she experienced the abuse in her relationship with her former partner, Melanie felt she couldn't cope with even the smallest of problems she faced in life. She had always believed herself to be a self-sufficient and competent person until she met her former partner when everything changed. Melanie was convinced she could no longer function well enough to move on with her life. She felt hopeless and adrift. Melanie's counsellor asked her to consider times she had coped with things in the past. Melanie told the counsellor about the breakdown of her relationship with the father of her daughter that occurred before she met her abusive partner. She recalled that it had been a difficult time, and she had been very sad but had done what she could to ensure her daughter felt secure and happy. She said she had established a home for them, got a job, arranged daycare for her daughter, and set herself up financially. She recalled feeling proud of her ability to ensure her daughter's well-being.*

Positive self-talk

Stop thinking in self-doubting and negative ways. Instead, engage in encouraging and positive thinking. This does not require you to say over-the-top and unrealistically positive things to yourself. Positive and encouraging self-talk, for example, may be something like, "I will do the best that I can."

> *It was pointed out to Celia by her counsellor that she was engaging in the type of self-talk that was likely to undermine her confidence and self-efficacy. Paying attention to what she was saying to herself, Celia realised her counsellor was right. So, she tried to change her thinking. She was kinder to herself. She recognised she was trying her hardest and could not expect more of herself. She praised herself for achieving her goals, even if they were small ones. Celia could see that this type of self-talk made her feel more settled and confident.*

Accept failures and learn from them

Recognise that it is unlikely that you will succeed in all you undertake. This is a normal part of life. We learn from our mistakes. These types of experiences cause us to make different choices in the future.

> *Michaela was frustrated. She was trying hard to get her life back in order, but things didn't always work out the way she had expected. She didn't get the job she wanted and missed out on the rental property she most wanted. She started to feel quite despondent, blaming herself for these failures. She began to tell herself she was hopeless and couldn't do what she set out to achieve. But Michaela's friends told her she was being unnecessarily harsh. So, she stopped and thought about what she was doing and how she was undermining herself by being so critical. Michaela took a deep breath and realised that everyone makes mistakes and fails to achieve what they want at some point in their lives. She gave some consideration to how she could do things differently so that she improved her chances of success. This required that she look at her 'failures' objectively rather than seeing them as evidence of her hopelessness.*

Seek feedback that is constructive

A lot of people will tell you what you should do. The flood of advice can be confusing and overwhelming. You need to remember that much of this advice is just the opinion of the advice giver and not 'the truth'. It is better to seek out constructive criticism from people you truly trust and who have a history of giving good advice.

> *Sarah was being pulled in lots of different directions. Everyone she spoke with about her situation had different advice for her. One person told her to take legal action to ensure her former partner was left with nothing. Another person told her she hadn't tried hard enough to make the relationship work. Sarah was given a different opinion about what she 'should do' whenever she turned to someone. So, Sarah decided to step back from all these confusing suggestions. She knew she needed to find ways to build her confidence to allow herself to move forward. Sarah decided to turn to the people who always had her best interests in mind, that is, her mother and father. She trusted them and knew they only wanted the best for her. She pushed away all the voices of others in her mind and listened only to the advice she received from her parents.*

Build a network of supportive people

Put together a support network of people who can offer you good support in your decision-making. These should be people who believe in you and will boost your confidence. These people can be friends and family, mentors and professionals, or a combination of all.

> *When Gemma's relationship with her abusive partner ended, she felt she was unable to cope and wouldn't be able to get her life on track. However, she also knew that she had to find a way to do what she needed to improve her life situation. She knew she needed help. So, she contacted a number of people to assist her with the things she knew she had to do. She sought out a financial counsellor at a welfare organisation to help her work out what she needed to do to be secure. She re-engaged with a person who had previously been a close and supportive friend, seeking and receiving moral support. She reached out to her family for comfort. She obtained a referral to a mental health counsellor and engaged in a therapeutic relationship with that person. As she thought of things she needed to do, she sought out people who could assist her in achieving her goals. She only selected people who would encourage her to take charge of her life rather than those who seemed to want to take over her life.*

Take small risks

It is all right to step outside your comfort zone and take small risks. Indeed, this is how you will build your confidence by achieving the goals you set. Remember that you do not have to take enormous risks. Smaller ones will increase your chances of succeeding, which is important in building confidence.

> *Since the end of her abusive relationship, Lynne has been trying to keep everything manageable in her life. She felt less anxious when she acted in a cautious manner. She stayed home and focused on managing her day-to-day demands of running her home. But Lynne realised that doing this wasn't helping her. Her confidence wasn't improving, and she just didn't trust her ability to do more than she was already doing. She knew she couldn't go on like this. So, the first thing Lynne did was accept an invitation from her sister to join her for lunch at a local café. Lynne thought she would feel really exposed in public and wouldn't feel comfortable, but it turned out that she had a nice time. She then asked an old friend if she wanted to go to the cinema with her. Lynne then looked online for a short training course that would interest her and selected one that introduced bookkeeping software, thinking this might help her when she was ready to apply for a job. As she started to do these things, Lynne realised they were becoming easier to do. She could feel her confidence building.*

Practice resilience

Find ways to bounce back when you have had to deal with difficult times. In this way, you can develop resilience. Resilience refers to the ability to recover from or withstand the challenges and difficulties you face.

> *Nicola knew the relationship she had with her abusive former partner had changed her. Even after the relationship ended, she had felt downtrodden. People who knew her before had commented that she was not the same happy person she had been earlier in her life. Nicola knew she had to make some decisions. She didn't want to be like this and feel like this for the rest of her life. She realised that any change had to come from inside herself. Nicola made up her mind she was going to confront life fully. She would find ways to meet life demands with courage, knowing that having courage didn't mean doing things without fear but doing them despite the fear. She was determined to be optimistic that she could have a good life in the future. Nicola decided that her best response to someone who had tried to subdue and diminish her was to refuse to be subdued or diminished. She knew this might be difficult to achieve, but she was determined to do her best nonetheless.*

Following these suggestions can help you build confidence in your ability to do what you want to do. Next, we need to examine ways you can stand up for yourself, a skill that might have been undermined by the abusive relationship you experienced.

Understand your rights

We are often not clear about our rights, particularly those that relate to our ability to take charge of our lives. Let's look at some of the mistaken assumptions we make that may be related to your current situation and then your legitimate rights. We will also consider how holding these mistaken assumptions might affect how you react following an abusive relationship and how abandoning the mistaken assumption may improve your situation.

Table 10: Mistaken assumptions, their consequences and your legitimate rights.

Mistaken assumption	*It is selfish to put your needs before the needs of others.*
Consequence	You may end up not receiving the help and support you need to deal with the emotional costs of the abuse you experienced. This is because you may not ask for help and support for yourself if other people are suffering as well or if you think others are too busy with their own lives.
Legitimate right	You have a right to put yourself first some of the time.
Outcome	Understanding your right may allow you to ask for the help and support you need at this difficult time. The extent to which a person can offer you help and support should be determined by them, not by you.
Mistaken assumption	*You shouldn't take up other's valuable time with your own problems.*
Consequence	No one knows you need help if you do not say so. As a consequence, you do not receive the help you need.
Legitimate right	You have a right to ask for help or emotional support.
Outcome	The people who care about you will understand you need help, and they can offer you help if they are able.
Mistaken assumption	*People don't want to hear you feel bad, so keep it to yourself.*
Consequence	Your feelings are never expressed, and you end up feeling bottled up and isolated.

Legitimate right	You have a right to feel and express pain.
Outcome	You will be able to feel some relief by sharing how you feel. Your emotional pain is not harmful to others who care about you. Friendships should be equal and reciprocal in that you should support your friends, and they should support you in times of distress. Accepting that people may be concerned about you frees you to express how you are feeling and allows your friends to do something for you at a time when it probably seems to them there is little they can do to make things better.
Mistaken assumption	*When someone takes the time to give you advice, you should take it seriously.*
Consequence	You may be overwhelmed by people telling you what to do. Unfortunately, one person's advice can conflict with another's, which only increases your confusion.
Legitimate right	You have a right to ignore the advice of others.
Outcome	You will come to realise that the advice people give you is only their opinion and the final decision will be yours to make. You should not then feel pressured to do what others demand or expect, especially if it contradicts with what you need.
Mistaken assumption	*You should always try to accommodate others. If you don't, they won't be there when you need them.*
Consequence	You will be so busy thinking about what others need that you will have no opportunity to consider your own needs.
Legitimate right	You have a right to say no.
Outcome	You are the only person who truly knows how you are feeling, so you need to decide what you can take on and what you cannot. By understanding that you have the right to say no, you can pay attention to your own needs when they are greater than the needs of others.

Mistaken assumption	*Don't be anti-social. People are going to think you don't like them if you say you'd rather be alone instead of with them*
Consequence	You will have no opportunity to have time by yourself to reflect on what has happened and how you are feeling if you give in to the demands of others to do what they are offering, thus ensuring people are around you all the time.
Legitimate right	You have a right to be alone, even if others would prefer your company.
Outcome	By understanding you have a right to time to yourself, you may be able to strike a good balance between being around others and being alone to deal with your thoughts and feelings.
Mistaken assumption	*You should have a good reason for what you feel and do.*
Consequence	You waste energy thinking about how you present yourself to others and worrying about what they think about you.
Legitimate right	You have a right not to have to justify yourself to others.
Outcome	Particularly at times of intense distress, you should be able to express yourself without having to explain yourself to others who may have chosen to do things differently if they were in your situation.
Mistaken assumption	*When someone is in trouble, you should help them.*
Consequence	This may cause you to ignore your own needs in favour of the needs of others. This can result in your needs never being met.
Legitimate right	You have a right not to take responsibility for someone else's problem.
Outcome	There are times in life when your needs exceed the needs of others, even if they are facing problems of their own. Understanding this may free you to focus on your own emotional reactions without worrying about the emotional responses of others.

Mistaken assumption	*It is not nice to put people off. If questioned, give an answer.*
Consequence	Believing you must answer people's questions, you may feel pressured to discuss things you do not want to discuss at times when you are not feeling able to discuss them.
Legitimate right	You have a right to choose not to respond to a situation.
Outcome	Curiosity on the part of the questioner does not give them the right to know or you an obligation to respond to their questioning. You are the person who decides what you disclose and when you disclose it. By accepting this, you can maintain your privacy if that is what you choose.

In many cases, asserting your legitimate rights is largely a matter of you accepting that these rights are legitimate and then calmly acting on that understanding. However, in other cases, it will require a response from you to a demand from someone else. Learning to be assertive can help you stand up for your rights.

Learn to be assertive

Another useful focus of our attention is on assertive communication. We need to consider your assertiveness skills because you are likely to be faced with many challenging interactions that occur after the abusive relationships end. These may include personal issues, such as negotiating matters related to the end of the relationship and more practical things, such as living arrangements, property settlements or, importantly, parenting arrangements if you have children. However, assertiveness skills may also be useful in a more general sense if your ability to assert yourself has been undermined by the abuse you experienced.

Assertiveness refers to standing up for your rights without trampling over the rights of others. Some people mistake assertiveness for aggressiveness which refers to the aggressive assertion of your rights irrespective of the rights of others. At the other extreme is passivity, where a person will not stand up for their own rights and allow others to walk over them.

So, the aim here is to teach you to stand up for your own rights without trampling all over the rights of other people. An assertive interpersonal style will allow you to negotiate for what you want without demanding it happen.

Asking for change

Firstly, we need to consider how to assertively solve problems by making reasonable requests for change or appropriate requests for what you would like to have happen. Many people find this difficult. They will start to make a request but are easily derailed by the deflection techniques used by the other person. Alternatively, they will start to make a request but are then affected by the annoyance they feel about the response of the other person. This step-by-step guide below is designed to help you plan ahead for how you are going to manage a request for change.

Define the problem situation

You should start by defining the problem you are facing. Do this by focusing on the facts of the matter and not your interpretation of the situation. You should do this by being as specific as possible. Avoid generalisations like "It's always the case…" or "Nothing ever goes right…". So, keep a narrow focus on the situation you have identified that you wish to change. Limit this to one problem at a time rather than bombarding the other person with a list of grievances.

> *Despite my repeated requests that you make arrangements for me or someone in my family to collect my belongings, this has not occurred.*

Describe how you are feeling

Here, you get a chance to describe how you feel about the situation. Remember, you are referring to how you feel and not how someone else *made* you feel. Be clear about the link between your feelings and the problem situation. Again, do not generalise to all situations or all problems.

Avoid blaming others. By blaming others, you put them on the defensive and little is ever resolved as a consequence. When you talk about how you are feeling, use what are called 'I messages'. That is, your descriptions of your feelings should start with something like "I feel…". No one can argue with you about this matter. They cannot say that you do not feel something that you have stated you feel. If you started with "You make me feel…", it is likely that the other person would argue that it was not their intention to make you feel that way, and if you do, that is your problem. Using 'I messages' allows you to avoid that type of discussion. In any case, you are the person who decides how you feel, and you should be able to relate that feeling to the other person.

This is a good opportunity to express your feelings. It is a mistake to assume that others know what you are thinking or feeling if you have not said so. If you have not said how you feel, the other person can do little more than guess. We make a mistake by assuming that someone who knows you well can 'mindread' and automatically know what you are thinking or feeling. Clear communication works much better than allowing others to guess.

> *I am disappointed that this arrangement hasn't been made and annoyed it has gone on for so long.*

Make your request for change

Here, you should make a statement about what you want to happen. You need to be brief. Do not turn your request into a lecture. Also, you need to be specific. Clearly state what you want rather than use terms that are not concrete. For example, it will not help to say, "I want you to leave me alone" because that is a generalised statement that can be interpreted in a multitude of ways. You would be better off saying, "I want you to stop contacting me by phone or on social media," or "I want you to stop driving past my house".

> *I want an arrangement made for me or one of my family members to collect my belongings this weekend, on either Saturday or Sunday.*

Outline possible positive consequences

If the other person does not initially want to agree with your request, you may point out the positive consequences that would follow from agreement. Do not make wild promises. Just focus on the positive things that are likely to happen from the change you are requesting. You are building the argument for what you want. For example, you could say, "I want you to remove my name from your lease. If you do this, I will agree to you keeping the furniture".

> *If I or a family member can collect my belongings this weekend, I will make no claims on household items that we jointly purchased.*

Outline potential negative consequences

If the other person is still reluctant to agree with what you are asking, you can outline for them the likely negative consequences if they choose not to comply with your wishes. Do not threaten. Simply state what you understand as the bad things that will happen if things do not change. For example, you could say, "I want you to stop driving past my house. If you continue to drive past, I will seek a legal solution by applying for a restraining order".

It is important to remember that you should only outline negative consequences that you are certain you are willing to follow through on. You, too, have to live with the negative consequences, so do not outline something you are unwilling to do or have happen.

> *If I am prevented from collecting my belongings because you fail to make an arrangement for me or a family member to do so, I will seek the assistance of the police to remove my possessions safely, and I will pursue a settlement regarding jointly purchased household items.*

So, to summarise, when making a request for change, do the following:

- Define the problem situation
- Describe how you are feeling
- Make your request for change
- Outline possible positive consequences
- Outline potential negative consequences

This is a good approach to standing up for your rights assertively. It is relatively simple and straightforward. You can also work out what you want to say in advance, and this protects you from having to make it up on the spot.

However, standing up for your rights may not be enough in itself if you are aiming for assertive communication. You need to be able to negotiate for what you want with a person who may be inclined not to give this to you. This might be any person in your life and not necessarily only your former partner. Consider the following negotiation process.

Negotiating for what you want

To negotiate with another person, your starting point needs to be that you both have needs that are equally important. This will require some effort on your part. It is easy for us to assume that what we want is right and what the other person wants is wrong. However, if you hold this view, any interaction about the issue in question will be an argument rather than a negotiation.

There are six steps that should be taken when you enter into a negotiation. Let's consider each of these steps.

Know what it is you want

Know what it is that you are negotiating for. You must have a clearly defined goal if you are to enter into a negotiation. If you are not clear about what you want, then how can the other person have any idea?

Make a statement of what you want in specific terms

In specific terms and being as clear as possible, make a statement about what you want or do not want to have happen. This can be in terms of what you want or do not want the other person to do. However, it may also be in terms of what you want as the outcome or end goal.

Listen to the point of view of the other person

Your aim here is to understand the other person's perspective. To do this, you have to listen carefully to what the other person has to say about their point of view. Rather than just passively listening, you should use active listening skills where you can ask for clarification or elaboration. Remember, you may not agree with the other person's perspective. What you should be doing is appreciating that they have a point of view that might be different from yours, but it is their point of view nonetheless.

Make a proposal

Next, you should make a proposal that offers a resolution. The proposal should not be solely based on what you want. It should take into account the other person's needs. This can be a challenging step that may take some thought on your part. It is easier to conceptualise a proposal that takes into account what both of you want if you approach it with the goal of achieving a 'win-win' outcome. This is where you get some of what you want, and the other person gets some of what they want. A win-win proposal has a much better chance of being accepted than a 'my way or the highway' approach.

Ask for a counterproposal

If your proposal is not accepted, do not be disheartened. Ask the other person for a counterproposal. Remember that your goal is to reach a point where you can both accept the proposal, even if you both do not get all of what you want.

Aim for compromise

The end result of any negotiation is typically a compromise. You are unlikely to get everything your way, but neither is the other person. You are aiming to reach a middle point that is satisfactory to you both. There are a variety of ways a compromise can be achieved:

> You give up some of what you want to gain some of what you want, and so does the other person.
>
> You might split the difference.
>
> You might agree that you do it your way when you are in control, and the other person does it their way when they are in control.

This last type of compromise can be useful when people cannot agree with parenting rules. In these cases, you might decide that you make the rules when the children are with you, and the other parent makes the rules when the children are with them.

Often at the end of a relationship there are issues that will have to be negotiated. You need to feel able to stand up for your rights and you need to be able to negotiate for an acceptable outcome. In doing this, you are aiming to move towards a satisfactory outcome so that you can move on with your life, unhindered by unresolved problems.

Improving the quality of your life

Undoubtedly, you are facing a difficult time recovering from the effects of the abuse you experienced and re-establishing your life. You are likely to feel adrift, not only because of the influence of the abuse but because you have disregarded your own needs for an extended period of time.

One thing that can happen as a result of spending a long time accommodating someone else's needs or being focused on surviving is that you lose sight of the things that you can do to please yourself. It is important that you have the opportunity to do some things for yourself. Having a balance between the tasks that are important that you undertake and some leisure time will improve the balance of your life.

It is important that you choose activities that are meaningful to you and that will improve the satisfaction you feel with your life. It is easy to fill your life with things to do, even leisure activities. However, not all of these potential activities will give you a sense of satisfaction. This is because not all activities are important to you. You should choose activities that are of high value to you if your goal is to make your life fuller *and* more meaningful.

How do you know what activities would contribute the most to improving the quality of your life? We often do not think about what we value as we go through our busy day and the question of what a person values can often be confounding to them. Borrowing from a particular therapy called Acceptance and Commitment Therapy, we have included here an exercise in values clarification that will help you decide which activities would be of the greatest value to you.

The goal of this exercise is to identify ways you can put into your life the things that you value the most. The purpose of doing this is to improve your quality of life by having more things in your life that matter to you the most.

When we refer to the things you value, we are not referring to a specific activity. For example, you may have a value related to spending more time with your family. A specific activity that might flow from this value is to have a meal with your family once a week.

Below is a diagram that contains labels for various life domains. A life domain is an area of your life that reflects one portion of who you are and what you do. This is an example of what we are talking about when we refer to your life domain map.

Values clarification exercise for choosing preferred activities

Step 1 involves you listing as many life domains as you can think of that are relevant to you. We have included some life domains that people often list, but feel free to change them and add new ones that reflect your life. What you are doing here is building your life domain map. Take your time to think up as many life domains as you understand to be part of your life. Other examples might be travel, exercise, etc.

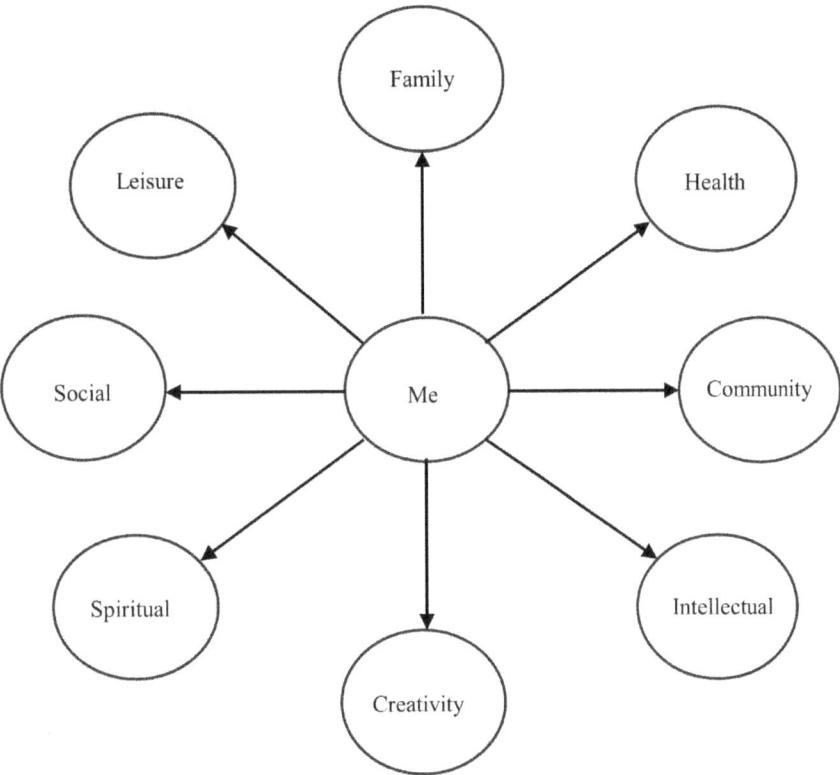

Figure 7: Example of a life domain map.

Step 2 involves you identifying what you already have in your life for the various life domains. Remember, list the values you have (e.g., ample time with my family) rather than specific activities (e.g., Sunday lunch with my family). You will begin to notice that some domains in your life have received lots of attention, but other domains have received little or no attention. Here is an example of the types of values that might appear in the family domain.

    Family domain:

        Time with family

        Special time with individual family members

        Spending time with the young members of my family

        Important family gatherings

Remember, you are listing here what you already have of value in your life with regard to this domain. This is not a list of the things you would like to have available to you.

Step 3 involves you now considering the things you would like to have in your life in each of the domains. Again, focus on the values (e.g., more quality time with my parents) rather than activities (e.g., visiting my parents on Sunday afternoons).

At this point, you will begin to notice several things.

You will see that there are domains of your life that have received lots of attention already, and you want very little else in that domain. Things in these domains are already satisfactory so there is limited purpose in focusing your attention on them.

You will see that there are domains of your life where you have very little but you also do not really want very much more. These do not deserve your attention either.

Importantly, you will see there are domains of your life where you have very little, and there are many things that you want in that domain that you do not already have available to you. Focusing your attention on these would give you the greatest benefit.

It is the third type of life domain that will become the focus of attention from here on. This is because this focus will have the greatest chance of having the most important impact on the quality of your life.

Step 4 involves focusing on those life domains where you do not have enough of what matters to you, and there is very much more that you want to include in your life. In this step, you should consider how those values that you want to put into your life might translate into specific activities. It is here that the 'what to do' component of the exercise occurs. For example, if you have a value associated with spending more time with your family, you might now consider ways that could happen by identifying specific activities you could engage in that would bring that value into your life (e.g., arranging family get-togethers, organising an online shared family photo site where family members can post photos for all family members to see).

Step 5 involves identifying any barriers that might prevent you from engaging in these activities that would bring the things that you value into your life and finding ways around these barriers. For example, you may not be able to catch up in person with family members if they live in places distant from you, but you could overcome this barrier by arranging video chat get-togethers.

Of course, there will be things you want that are of value to you that you just cannot have because of real limitations. For example, you may like to travel, but you cannot do so because you cannot afford the expense. However, if travel is of high value, then the quality of your life might be enhanced by spending time exploring places online or watching travel documentaries. Although not exactly what you would give the highest value, these activities are still related to the thing that matters to you.

Remember that your goal is to introduce into your life activities that are of high value to you that will improve the quality of your life. If you are going to devote the time to engaging in these types of activities, it will matter that you focus on the activities that are associated with your highest values.

Some final points

There are a number of points that need to be made or restated.

No one deserves to be abused by an intimate partner. This is true no matter what your former partner told you or led you to believe. Violence towards a partner, in any form, is not an appropriate way for anyone to communicate their needs, express their displeasure or exert control and influence.

The experience of abuse in an intimate relationship can have profound psychological effects. Everyone is vulnerable to these types of effects. Even people who functioned well psychologically before the relationship can still be harmed by intimate partner abuse.

You are not to blame for the behaviour of another person. Your former partner chose to behave the way he did, and you should not take responsibility for his actions.

Many people, probably the majority, have an odd tendency to feel guilty for things over which they genuinely have no control. If you have knowingly done something to harm someone, you should feel guilty. However, it is not appropriate to feel guilt for someone else's choices or behaviour. Choose a different, more accurate emotional response to what has happened. For example, you might feel disappointment that the abuse happened, resentment that you had to go through those experiences, regret that you did not walk away sooner, or even compassion for the abuser because of the problems with which he was obviously burdened. However, do not feel guilt for another person's poor choices and behaviour. All of these alternative and more accurate emotional states are legitimate and are much more manageable psychologically than guilt.

Your future should not be determined by the abuse you experienced. After you leave a relationship, the risk of abuse diminishes, and with every passing day, your abusive experiences increasingly become historical events in your life and not your current circumstance. Dwelling on the 'what if…' and 'if only…' in relation to the abusive relationship just keeps you in a past you have no power to change. Learn to accept what has happened and look forward to a better future. Remember that it is not what happened to you that will determine the future but what you choose to do about the effect on you of the abuse. Choose a better future.

It is possible to have a good future and a new, loving relationship with a different person. Understand that a good quality relationship is characterised by equality and reciprocity and not power-imbalance, control and aggression.

In the aftermath of an abusive relationship, it is easy to believe you would find it impossible to trust anyone and allow yourself to be vulnerable. However, it is worth remembering that trust is earned. All that is required of you is that, when you are ready, you give a person the opportunity to demonstrate to you that they are trustworthy and allow them the chance to act in ways that will earn your trust.

We wish you all the best for the future.

Additional readings

Eifer, G.H., Forsyth, J.P., & Hayes, S.C. (2005). *Acceptance and commitment therapy for anxiety disorders.* New York: New Harbinger Publications.

Kennerley, H., Kirk, J., & Westbrook, D. (2016). *An introduction to cognitive behaviour therapy: Skills and applications (3rd edn.).* London: Sage Publications.

Paterson, R.J. (2023). *The assertiveness workbook: How to express your ideas and stand up for yourself at work and in relationships.* London: New Harbinger Publications.

Sears, R.W. (2021). *The sense of self: Perspectives from science and Zen Buddhism.* Springer Nature.

Tobin, D., Holroyd, K., Reynolds, R., & Wigal, J.K. (1989). The hierarchical structure of the Coping Strategies Inventory. *Cognitive Therapy and Research, 13(4),* 343-361.

www.ingramcontent.com/pod-product-compliance
Lightning Source LLC
Chambersburg PA
CBHW081522160426

43195CB00015B/2473